W O R D P L A Y

--·——·-- ·for Kids· --·——·--

WORDPLAY
for Kids

A Sourcebook *of* Poems, Rhymes, *and* Read-Alouds

TIM WADHAM

An imprint of the American Library Association
CHICAGO 2015

Tim Wadham is the director of the Puyallup Public Library, in Puyallup, Washington. Previously, he was youth services coordinator for the Maricopa County Library District, in Phoenix, Arizona. Since 2002, he has been an adjunct professor for the University of Arizona Library School, teaching courses in children's literature and youth services. He is also a children's author and published his first picture book, *The Queen of France*, with Candlewick Press in 2011. He has written two titles for the professional market with Neal-Schuman, including *Libros esenciales*, a guide to creating and programming a core collection of Spanish-language and bilingual materials.

ISBN: 978-0-8389-1266-9 (paper)

Library of Congress Cataloging-in-Publication Data
Wadham, Tim.
    Wordplay for kids : a sourcebook of poems, rhymes, and read-alouds / Tim Wadham.
      pages cm
    Includes bibliographical references and index.
    ISBN 978-0-8389-1266-9 (print : alk. paper) 1. Children's libraries—Activity programs—United States. 2. Poetry—Study and teaching (Elementary)—Activity programs. 3. Children's literature—Study and teaching (Elementary)—Activity programs. 4. Language arts (Elementary)—Activity programs. 5. Children's poetry—Bibliography. 6. Children's literature—Bibliography. I. Title.
Z718.3W33 2015

   027.62'5—dc23

                               2014025358

Book design by Kimberly Thornton in the Charis SIL and Adelle typefaces.

♾ This paper meets the requirements of ANSI/NISO Z39.48–1992 (Permanence of Paper).

Printed in the United States of America

19 18 17 16 15   5 4 3 2 1

To Katie Blake and Cynthia Daniels.
Also to Bonnie Anderson and Carol Hopkins
who developed several of the after-school
programs in this book.

CONTENTS

FOREWORD

THE IDEA FOR THIS BOOK BEGAN IN 1985. I HAD JUST COMPLETED MY master's degree in library science. While I was looking for a full-time, professional position, I spent a year working as a part-time public library clerk and a part-time school library aide. It was in the school library, under the tutelage of an outstanding school librarian named Katie Blake that I experienced a program that has influenced, to this day, my approach to literature-based programs and activities in public libraries.

One benefit of working in a school library setting is the potential of having a captive audience you can impact on a regular, usually weekly basis. Katie Blake took advantage of this opportunity and created a program she originally called Childread—in her words, "an attempt to organize that gigantic subject, children's literature, so that it may be introduced in a systematic way during weekly 'library' time." As her aide, I was able to spend a year implementing this program, which is really quite elegant in its simplicity. As classes came in for their scheduled time, they would sit down on steps in a sunken kiva-like area, and we would start with choral poetry reading. The poems were written on a large easel pad so that the kids could read along together out loud. We would follow up with a few books with the younger grades or a chapter from a book for the upper grades. Then there would be an activity based on the book. Being involved with this program for almost an entire school year allowed me to see the impact of the program over time. What I saw happening that year was really quite remarkable. Of course, the children memorized the poems, but as they did so, I could see a progression in their literacy skills over the year. The improvement in their vocabulary and verbal skills was visible.

Knowing that I was going into public librarianship, I began to wonder how I could achieve the same results in a public library setting, where I did not have the benefit of a captive audience. The answer came in the form of another wonderful school librarian, Cynthia Daniels, who approached me after I began work at the Dallas West branch of the Dallas Public Library in Texas. She had just received a grant and asked if I would be willing to create an after-school program to which she and another school librarian could bring children two days a week. My thoughts immediately went to adapting Katie Blake's program for a public library setting. The kids began coming twice a week. I began the program just as I had done in the school library, with choral poetry reading. Since these kids were mid- to upper-elementary age, I would read a chapter of a book each time they came. Most memorably, we made it through *The Whipping Boy,* by Sid Fleischman. When I suggested the book, Cynthia and her coworker were skeptical. West Dallas was the most economically disadvantaged community in the entire city, and I was working with minority students who lived in a massive government-housing project. The librarians weren't sure that a book about a prince in an inferred eighteenth-century setting would have any relevance for their kids. *The Whipping Boy* turned out to be one of the favorites of all the books we read over the three years I ran the program in West Dallas. I believe it was because although the setting of the book was admittedly far removed from the daily reality of these kids from the projects, it resonated with them on a more universal level because of the idea of the whipping boy himself: every kid can relate to the trauma of being punished for something you didn't do.

I did not see the real impact of this program until fourteen years later, when one of the kids from the after-school group came into the branch library where I was then working in Dallas and remembered that I used to read books to him. He was now an adult, using the library and reading to his own children.

During my years in Dallas, from there to Arizona, and now in Washington State, I have continued to successfully use variations of this program, even when there were not school librarians with a grant to transport their students twice a week. This has become my go-to style of programming, and I have done entire sessions on one book, the work of a specific author, or different activities each week connected by a common theme, such as fantasy or mysteries.

Developed as a companion program to Childread, Shared Warmth was a program that Katie Blake developed as a way to extend the program beyond the school library to a child's parents or caregiver, and as a way to encourage parents to read out loud to their children. Chapter 1 of *Wordplay for Kids* describes a new take on implementing the Shared Warmth concept in a public library setting.

The original Childread program was arranged sequentially by grade level. Since it would be difficult to create public library programs restricted to grade levels, this book is divided into two basic sections with suggested poems, books, and programs for five- to seven-year-olds and eight- to twelve-year-olds.

The emphasis of chapter 2 of *Wordplay for Kids,* for ages five to seven, is to help children develop a "literary ear": artful language patterns, correct and interesting language usage (grammar), and a large and rich vocabulary. *Wordplay for Kids* features almost 100 nursery rhymes and a great deal of poetry designed to share orally. Because of copyright issues, the texts of most poems not in the public domain are not included. However, I have included multiple ways to find sources for the text of as many of these poems as possible, both online and in books and anthologies. As in traditional storytimes for preschool children, a major focus for younger students is to listen to books read out loud. Children of this age are ready to move on from simple picture books and can be challenged with more complex stories, including folklore and fables. I include lists of recommended picture books, easy fiction, and fiction that can be shared. My experience with this age group is that we should never underestimate the ability of children to understand and respond to literature that we might think is too difficult. I was introduced to Greek mythology in the second grade through the Sullivan Programmed Reading curriculum, which made a huge impact on me at the time. Suggestions for introducing Greek mythology are included here, along with some recommended collections. I have also included one sample program for this age group, based on the fourteen Oz books by L. Frank Baum, as an example of a way to use longer, chapter-length books with five- to seven-year-olds. Reading out loud should always be followed by a chance for children to participate in activities, such as creative dramatization, visual art, or music activities, directly based on the books just shared. A central goal of *Wordplay* is to help children lose their video-game passivity and turn them into active participants.

Chapter 3 of *Wordplay for Kids,* for ages eight to twelve, features poems, most of which are short, many humorous, and all selected with kid appeal in mind. The poems are divided into categories, including classic, longer narrative poems. Although it might seem at first glance that some of these longer poems might not be appropriate for this age group, I would note as above never to underestimate a child's ability to understand. Also, since the purpose of the Wordplay program is to make children familiar with unfamiliar words and more complex and rich language, challenging children with longer narrative poetry can make a huge impact on their vocabulary and literacy skills. Book lists that introduce children to more advanced fairy-tale adaptations and folktales are included in addition to a recommended fiction book list. The primary way of presenting these books is through reading them aloud in a *Wordplay for Kids* session. Titles can also be presented using booktalks and media. Finally, a series of sample after-school program ideas are presented, all of which have been successfully used in the field.

This book is not just for public librarians working with children. It is for school librarians, who I hope will begin utilizing this program as it was presented in its original setting. It is for homeschoolers and their parents and teachers as well, and it can easily be adapted as a way of creating a literature curriculum for homeschool support groups. I believe in this program. I believe that it can make a real and lasting difference in the lives of children. It will help create a love of poetry and the sound and rhythm of language. As children's facility with oral language improves, their vocabulary as well as their writing skills will also be strengthened. The books and stories to which they are exposed will provide an essential element of cultural literacy that will serve them all their life. *Wordplay for Kids* is presented with the purpose of helping children want to read; to encourage them to be lifelong readers; and, by being familiar with literature's wide range of experiences, to be sensitive, informed, and loving human beings.

Katie Blake passed away on November 26, 2012. Although she is not able to see this project come to fruition, she did give full permission for me to use her original Childread materials and expressed great enthusiasm when I let her know that this book was under contract. A statement in her obituary reads: "Of particular delight to her was her students' mastery of nursery rhymes and tongue twisters. She called it setting their ear to the language." It will be a fitting tribute if those who use this program can develop a similar love and mastery of the language with the students who participate.

Chapter 1

Shared Warmth

A Parent-Child Reading Program

•·————————·•

AS PART OF LIBRARIAN KATIE BLAKE'S CHILDREAD program, introducing children to literature, she also implemented a reading program that involved parents that she called Shared Warmth. The Shared Warmth program encourages families to read together. The success of Shared Warmth caused the program to be implemented in other schools and to be included as a recommended program in M. Ellen Jay and Hilda L. Jay's *Ready-to-Go Reading Incentive Programs for Schools and Libraries* (New York: Neal-Schuman, 1998).

Philosophy behind Shared Warmth

What makes the difference between a person who identifies him- or herself as someone who loves to read, someone who is a voracious reader, or someone who never chooses to read but reads only what is required? Why did that person become one type of reader instead of the other?

You will find, almost without exception, that people who love to read attribute that love to the home. Either their mother or their father or both read to them regularly. Parents who read a lot themselves typically provide books in the home for their children as well.

Teachers and librarians, though they have the power to be highly influential in creating readers, can never be as influential as parents. So what can a public library do? Public libraries face lots of challenges with children who come into the library as well as children who must be reached by going outside the walls of the physical building. Children have video-game and electronics-induced passivity. Often, one or both parents are working and have little time to interact with their children. What can the public library do to capture attention? This is where Shared Warmth comes in. Libraries need to develop a family/home/library reading program.

What Is Shared Warmth?

Shared Warmth's family/home/library reading program is what *Wordplay for Kids* is reaching for—a climate where the love of reading is fostered by parents, children, and public librarians together. Shared Warmth is reading done at home, not only by the child, but also by the parent reading to the child or vice versa. That is the key. It is such a simple thing, but there is no question that one of the very best things that parents can do for their children from day one is to simply read to them out loud.

Requirements, Recognition, and Record Keeping

To kick off a library's Shared Warmth program, parents are invited to attend a special "Back to School/Back to the Library" night. While children's librarians provide a storytime that includes choral poetry reading and activities for the children in a separate location, the parents attend a session explaining the Shared Warmth program and detailing the importance of reading aloud to their children and of having books in the home. At such a program, librarians can also demonstrate booktalks for the parents. Librarians can make sure that everyone is registered for library cards. Next, the children come back into the room with their parents and, for example, perform a short poem that they learned in the storytime. At the end of the program, each child may receive a book of his or her own to take home, and each family receives a Shared Warmth calendar. Any calendar can be used, or even a printout of a month, so parents and kids can write on it.

On the calendar, the parent or guardian initials each day when one of the following is accomplished:

1. Parent reads to the child
2. Child reads to the parent
3. Child reads silently

Public libraries can set a specific length of time for the program and come up with the required reading time. Five- to seven-year-olds may only need to read or be read to fifteen minutes a night. Eight- to ten-year-olds might be challenged to read twenty to thirty minutes. Eleven- and twelve-year-olds could be reading thirty minutes or more per night.

Required reading nights are Mondays through Fridays, and if a night is missed, Saturday or Sunday can be used as makeup days. This means that children and parents should be participating in Shared Warmth twenty-one to twenty-two days per month.

The child or parents should return their Shared Warmth calendar to the library for the previous month on a designated day, such as the third working day of each month. Parents should initial each day the goal was met on the calendar. Children who return the calendar with the required days checked off could have their names (first name and last initial) displayed prominently in the children's area of the library.

There should be a reward each month for children who complete the required days. This reading incentive can take almost any form—coupons, a book or DVD, candy—whatever works for your community and your budget.

When Shared Warmth is conducted in a school setting, it takes place during the school year—from August or September to May or June. In a public library setting, it can also span the school year. Children who complete the required nine months can be honored at an end-of-the-year party at the library. They can receive specially designed T-shirts, have their names engraved on a plaque permanently placed in the library, and be featured in a group photo. This sort of program, done correctly, can challenge students and truly galvanize both the parents and the larger community.

The original Shared Warmth program had an incredible response. Parents were checking out books. Parents loved doing Shared Warmth and the new quiet reading time in the evening. Parents mentioned that some children would not go to bed without doing their reading time and having their calendars initialed. From a statistical standpoint, the local school's achievement tests showed significant increases, particularly with the ten- to twelve-year-olds.

Libraries doing Shared Warmth might also find other ways to provide positive reinforcement to children who are participating in the program. Children's librarians need to reach those children who might not have any encouragement to read at home and whose parents are not interested in Shared Warmth.

> We can't expect our young people, in their most sensitive, formative years, to love what we do not love, or to value what we do not value. Facts go into our brain cells. Living examples go into our bone marrow. A child caught up in the joy of reading is marvelous; even better are the moments when young and

old share the joy together. There's no happier combination, and that indeed may be the only magic formula.   —*Lloyd Alexander*

To facilitate that magic combination between child and parent or adult is at its heart the goal of Shared Warmth.

Wordplay for
Five- to Seven-Year-Olds

HIS CHAPTER OF *WORDPLAY FOR KIDS* PROVIDES resources for introducing younger children, ages five to seven, to literature in a public library or school library setting. The materials provide a great deal of flexibility for programmers to develop a variety of programs for a variety of audiences and settings, including homeschools. This style of programming is meant to be a next step after preschool storytimes. Although these programs may include some elements that will be familiar to storytime kids, they should also feel different. The resource sections are in the order in which they are most effectively used in programming. When introducing any of these types of literature, children should be given the context of the form that they are hearing. For example, they should know that fables are a type of story that includes a moral.

I. Poetry for Choral Reading

Programs should always begin with choral poetry reading. This activity is one of the most defining and unique features of this style of programming. It is also crucial to achieve the potential literacy benefits. The text of the poems should be either projected on a screen or written on a large notepad placed on an easel. The text should be large enough for young children to be able to read from where they are sitting. An alternative could be to provide children with a printed handout with the text of the poems from which they can read.

II. Nursery Rhymes for Choral Reading

The inclusion of nursery rhymes serves another central purpose of this programming, which is to introduce children to classic literature, in whatever form. It is possible that many children might never hear these rhymes unless they are introduced to them in a library setting. *Wordplay for Kids* provides the opportunity for children to not only hear these rhymes, but also to say them out loud. The nursery rhymes are presented in three sets, with the idea that each set contains enough poems for children to master during a multiweek Wordplay program. When children have mastered one set, you can move on to the next. There are some rhymes that are repeated from one set to the next.

Hearing and saying these poems out loud will give children a greater appreciation for the fun of language: sound, rhyme, and rhythm.

III. Folktales and Fairy Stories

Children should be introduced to the original versions of the classic folktales and fairy stories. This prepares them not only with general cultural literacy, but also helps them better appreciate the many popular "fractured" fairy tales. Many children now become familiar with folktales and fairy stories through the postmodern versions, like *The Stinky Cheese Man* and *The Three Little Wolves and the Big Bad Pig*. The book list includes some of the most well-known tales. It includes a list of different versions of specific tales and a further list of individual folktales. The list also includes some of the classic versions and retellings in picture-book form.

IV. Fables

Fables are also an important part of folk literature to which children ought to be introduced. Because, as opposed to fairy tales and folktales, fables have such a distinctive form, they merit a separate program. Also, there are new fables to which children can be introduced along with the classic Aesop fables.

V. Greek Mythology

Learning Greek mythology is a crucial part of cultural literacy. This section gives an outline of myths and mythical characters from the Greeks and books that can be used to introduce this important legacy to children.

VI. Picture Books and Easy Fiction

The list of recommended picture books and easy fiction includes picture books and easy readers that can be shared in an after-school, home, or school library setting with the post-preschool storytime crowd.

VII. Fiction

As kids learn to read better, they are also prepared for more thematically complex stories, regardless of length. This list presents some recommended titles.

VIII. Sample Program: Discover the Oz Books

Books like *The Wizard of Oz* can be effectively introduced to children as early as age two or three as read-alouds. I was first introduced to Oz when I was five years old, and my mother purchased a set of all fourteen of L. Frank Baum's Oz books for Christmas. I still remember being downstairs and hearing her call, then running upstairs to find the box full of books. She began reading them out loud to me, and it is from them I taught myself to read. I also remember reading one of them to my baby sister and stopping in the middle of a sentence when I suddenly had the awareness that I was actually reading. Reading the Oz books aloud has great appeal for younger children.

I. Poetry for Choral Reading

Every session of choral poetry should begin with the following poem, by Beatrice Schenk de Regniers. This is a perfect poem to demonstrate the delight of poetry and the rhythm and the sound of the words. Make this the entry point for choral poetry reading.

"Keep a Poem in Your Pocket"   *by Beatrice Schenk de Regniers*

Keep a poem in your pocket
And a picture in your head
And you'll never feel lonely
At night when you're in bed.

The little poem will sing to you
The little picture bring to you
A dozen dreams to dance to you
At night when you're in bed.

So—
Keep a picture in your pocket
And a poem in your head
And you'll never feel lonely
At night when you're in bed.

This poem can be found in the following:
Austin, Mary C., and Queenie B. Mills. *The Sound of Poetry.* Boston: Allyn
and Bacon, 1963.
Larrick, Nancy. *Piping down the Valleys Wild: Poetry for the Young of All
Ages.* Illus. by Ellen Raskin. New York: Bantam Doubleday Dell Books
for Young Readers, 1999.
Prelutsky, Jack, ed. *The Random House Book of Poetry for Children.* Illus. by
Arnold Lobel. New York: Random House, 1983.

"Calling All Readers"   *by Laura Purdie Salas*

First lines: "I'll tell you a story. / I'll spin you a rhyme"

This poem can be found in the following:
Salas, Laura Purdie. *Bookspeak! Poems About Books.* Illus. by Josée Bisail-
lon. Boston: Clarion/Houghton Mifflin Harcourt, 2011.

Topic: Nature and Seasons

"Mud"   *by Polly Chase Boyden*

First line: "Mud is very nice to feel"

This poem can be found in the following:
Arbuthnot, May Hill, and Shelton L. Root, eds. *Time for Poetry: A Repre-
sentative Collection of Poetry for Children, to Be Used in the Classroom,
Home, or Camp; Especially Planned for College Classes in Children's Litera-
ture.* Illus. by Arthur Paul. Glenview, IL: Scott, Foresman, 1967.
Austin, Mary C., and Queenie B. Mills. *The Sound of Poetry.* Boston: Allyn
and Bacon, 1963.
Cole, Joanna. *A New Treasury of Children's Poetry: Old Favorites and New
Discoveries.* Illus. by Judith Gwyn Brown. Garden City, NY: Doubleday,
1984.
Gannett, Lewis. *The Family Book of Verse.* New York: Harper, 1961.

Prelutsky, Jack, ed. *The Random House Book of Poetry for Children*. Illus. by Arnold Lobel. New York: Random House, 1983.

Prelutsky, Jack, ed. *Read-Aloud Rhymes for the Very Young*. Illus. by Marc Brown. New York: Knopf, 1986.

"The Swing" *by Robert Louis Stevenson*

How do you like to go up in a swing,
Up in the air so blue?
Oh, I do think it the pleasantest thing
Ever a child can do!

Up in the air and over the wall,
Till I can see so wide,
Rivers and trees and cattle and all
Over the countryside—

Till I look down on the garden green,
Down on the roof so brown—
Up in the air I go flying again,
Up in the air and down!

This poem can be found in the following:

Stevenson, Robert Louis. *A Child's Garden of Verses*. Illus. by Michael Foreman. New York: Delacorte, 1985.

"I'm Glad the Sky Is Painted Blue" *—Anon.*

I'm glad the sky is painted blue
And the earth is painted green,
And such a lot of nice fresh air
All sandwiched in-between.

"Winter Clothes" *by Karla Kuskin*

First line: "Under my hood I have a hat"

This poem can be found in the following:

Prelutsky, Jack, ed. *The Random House Book of Poetry for Children*. Illus. by Arnold Lobel. New York: Random House, 1983.

"The More It Snows"   *by A. A. Milne*

First lines: "The more it / SNOWS-tiddely-pom"

This poem can be found in the following:
> Cole, Joanna. *A New Treasury of Children's Poetry: Old Favorites and New Discoveries.* Illus. by Judith Gwyn Brown. Garden City, NY: Doubleday, 1984.
>
> de Regniers, Beatrice Schenk, ed. *Sing a Song of Popcorn: Every Child's Book of Poems.* Illus. by Marcia Brown. New York: Scholastic, 1988.
>
> Milne, A. A. *The House at Pooh Corner.* Illus. by Ernest H. Shepard. New York: Dutton, 1961.
>
> Prelutsky, Jack, ed. *The Random House Book of Poetry for Children.* Illus. by Arnold Lobel. New York: Random House, 1983.
>
> Prelutsky, Jack, ed. *Read-Aloud Rhymes for the Very Young.* Illus. by Marc Brown. New York: Knopf, 1986.
>
> Royds, Caroline. *Poems for Young Children.* Illus. by Inga Moore. Garden City, NY: Doubleday, 1986.

"Maytime Magic"   *by Mabel Watts*

First lines: "A little seed / for me to sow?"

This poem can be found in the following:
> Prelutsky, Jack, ed. *The Random House Book of Poetry for Children.* Illus. by Arnold Lobel. New York: Random House, 1983.

"Yellow"   *by David McCord*

First lines: "Green is go / and red is stop"

This poem can be found in the following:
> Prelutsky, Jack, ed. *The Random House Book of Poetry for Children.* Illus. by Arnold Lobel. New York: Random House, 1983.

Topic: People and Things

"Antigonish"   *by Hughes Mearns*

> Yesterday upon the stair
> I met a man who wasn't there
> He wasn't there again today
> I wish, I wish he'd go away

When I came home last night at three
The man was waiting there for me
But when I looked around the hall
I couldn't see him there at all!

Go away, go away, don't you come back any more!
Go away, go away, and please don't slam the door

Last night I saw upon the stair
A little man who wasn't there
He wasn't there again today
Oh, how I wish he'd go away

This poem can be found in the following:
Wikipedia, at http://en.wikipedia.org/wiki/William_Hughes_Mearns.

"Our Washing Machine"   *by Patricia Hubbell*

First lines: "Our washing machine went / whisity whirr"

This poem can be found in the following:
Prelutsky, Jack, ed. *The Random House Book of Poetry for Children.* Illus. by
Arnold Lobel. New York: Random House, 1983.

"If Things Grew Down"   *by Robert D. Hoeft*

If things grew down instead of up,
A dog would grow into a pup.
A cat would grow into a kitten,
Your sweater would grow into a mitten.

A cow would grow into a calf,
A whole would grow into a half.
Big would grow into something small,
And small would grow into nothing at all!

"Halfway Down"   *by A. A. Milne*

First lines: "Halfway down the stairs / is a stair / where I sit"

This poem can be found in the following:
Milne, A. A. *When We Were Very Young.* Illus. by Ernest H. Shepard. New
York: Dutton, 1961.

"The Pickety Fence" *by David McCord*

First line: "The pickety fence"

This poem can be found in the following:
> Arbuthnot, May Hill, and Shelton L. Root, eds. *Time for Poetry: A Representative Collection of Poetry for Children, to Be Used in the Classroom, Home, or Camp; Especially Planned for College Classes in Children's Literature.* Illus. by Arthur Paul. Glenview, IL: Scott, Foresman, 1967.
>
> Cole, Joanna. *A New Treasury of Children's Poetry: Old Favorites and New Discoveries.* Illus. by Judith Gwyn Brown. Garden City, NY: Doubleday, 1984.

Topic: Thoughts for Growing

"Advice to Small Children" *by Edward Anthony*

First lines: "Eat no green apples / or you'll droop"

This poem can be found in the following:
> Prelutsky, Jack, ed. *The Random House Book of Poetry for Children.* Illus. by Arnold Lobel. New York: Random House, 1983.

"Always Finish" —Anon.

> If a task is once begun,
> Never leave it 'til it's done.
> Be the labor great or small,
> Do it well or not at all.

Topic: Halloween

"Three Little Ghostesses" —Mother Goose

> Three little ghostesses
> Sitting on postesses
> Eating buttered toastesses,
> Greasing their fistesses
> Up to their wristesses.
> Oh, what beastesses,
> To make such feastesses.

"The Hidebehind" *by Michael Rosen*

First line: "Have you seen the Hidebehind?"

This poem can be found in the following:
> Fisher, Robert. *Amazing Monsters: Verses to Thrill and Chill.* Illus. by
> Rowena Allen. London: Faber and Faber, 1982.

"Wanted—a Witch's Cat" *by Shelagh McGee*

First lines: "Wanted—a witch's cat. / Must have vigor and spite"

This poem can be found in the following:
> Chapman, Jean. *Cat Will Rhyme with Hat: A Book of Poems.* Illus. by Peter
> Parnall. New York: Scribner, 1986.
> Prelutsky, Jack, ed. *The Random House Book of Poetry for Children.* Illus. by
> Arnold Lobel. New York: Random House, 1983.

Topic: Thanksgiving

"The New-England Boy's Song about Thanksgiving Day" —*L. Maria Child*

> Over the river, and through the wood,
> To grandfather's house we go;
> The horse knows the way,
> To carry the sleigh,
> Through the white and drifted snow.

> Over the river, and through the wood,
> To grandfather's house away!
> We would not stop
> For doll or top,
> For 't is Thanksgiving day.

> Over the river, and through the wood,
> Oh, how the wind does blow!
> It stings the toes,
> And bites the nose,
> As over the ground we go.

> Over the river, and through the wood,
> With a clear blue winter sky,
> The dogs do bark,
> And children hark,
> As we go jingling by.

Over the river, and through the wood,
To have a first-rate play—
Hear the bells ring
Ting a ling ding,
Hurra for Thanksgiving day!

Over the river, and through the wood—
No matter for winds that blow;
Or if we get
The sleigh upset,
Into a bank of snow.

Over the river, and through the wood,
To see little John and Ann;
We will kiss them all,
And play snow-ball,
And stay as long as we can.

Over the river, and through the wood,
Trot fast, my dapple grey!
Spring over the ground,
Like a hunting hound,
For 't is Thanksgiving day!

Over the river, and through the wood,
And straight through the barn-yard gate;
We seem to go
Extremely slow,
It is so hard to wait.

Over the river, and through the wood,
Old Jowler hears our bells;
He shakes his pow,
With a loud bow wow,
And thus the news he tells.

Over the river, and through the wood—
When grandmother sees us come,
She will say, Oh dear,
The children are here,
Bring a pie for every one.

Over the river, and through the wood—
Now grandmother's cap I spy!
Hurra for the fun!

Is the pudding done?
Hurra for the pumpkin pie!

"Attitude of Gratitude"   *by Val C. Wilcox*

There are reasons to be thankful everywhere around.
I am thankful for each blessing, here are some I've found:
I'm thankful for the daily food that I have to eat,
I'm thankful for my home, for neighbors on the street.

An attitude of gratitude
Will see good before the bad;
An attitude of gratitude
Is finding reasons to be glad.
I'm thankful for good people, friends and family.
I am thankful just for living, grateful to be me.

I'm thankful for the love that only I can share,
I'm thankful for my Heavenly Father always there.
An attitude of gratitude
Will see good before the bad;
An attitude of gratitude
Is finding reasons to be glad.

Topic: Christmas

"Christmas Is Coming"   *—Mother Goose*

Christmas is coming, the goose is getting fat.
Please to put a penny in the old man's hat.
If you haven't got a penny, a h'penny will do.
If you haven't got a h'penny then God bless you.

"A Visit from St. Nicholas"   *by Clement Clarke Moore*

'Twas the night before Christmas, when all through the house
Not a creature was stirring, not even a mouse;
The stockings were hung by the chimney with care,
In hopes that St. Nicholas soon would be there;

The children were nestled all snug in their beds;
While visions of sugar-plums danced in their heads;

And mamma in her 'kerchief, and I in my cap,
Had just settled our brains for a long winter's nap,

When out on the lawn there arose such a clatter,
I sprang from my bed to see what was the matter.
Away to the window I flew like a flash,
Tore open the shutters and threw up the sash.

The moon on the breast of the new-fallen snow,
Gave a lustre of midday to objects below,
When what to my wondering eyes did appear,
But a miniature sleigh and eight tiny rein-deer,

With a little old driver so lively and quick,
I knew in a moment he must be St. Nick.
More rapid than eagles his coursers they came,
And he whistled, and shouted, and called them by name:

"Now, Dasher! now, Dancer! now Prancer and Vixen!
On, Comet! on, Cupid! on, Donder and Blixen!
To the top of the porch! to the top of the wall!
Now dash away! dash away! dash away all!"

As leaves that before the wild hurricane fly,
When they meet with an obstacle, mount to the sky;
So up to the housetop the coursers they flew
With the sleigh full of toys, and St. Nicholas too—

And then, in a twinkling, I heard on the roof
The prancing and pawing of each little hoof.
As I drew in my head, and was turning around,
Down the chimney St. Nicholas came with a bound.

He was dressed all in fur, from his head to his foot,
And his clothes were all tarnished with ashes and soot;
A bundle of toys he had flung on his back,
And he looked like a peddler just opening his pack.

His eyes—how they twinkled! his dimples, how merry!
His cheeks were like roses, his nose like a cherry!
His droll little mouth was drawn up like a bow,
And the beard on his chin was as white as the snow;

The stump of a pipe he held tight in his teeth,
And the smoke, it encircled his head like a wreath;
He had a broad face and a little round belly
That shook when he laughed, like a bowl full of jelly.

He was chubby and plump, a right jolly old elf,
And I laughed when I saw him, in spite of myself;
A wink of his eye and a twist of his head
Soon gave me to know I had nothing to dread;

He spoke not a word, but went straight to his work,
And filled all the stockings; then turned with a jerk,
And laying his finger aside of his nose,
And giving a nod, up the chimney he rose;

He sprang to his sleigh, to his team gave a whistle,
And away they all flew like the down of a thistle.
But I heard him exclaim, ere he drove out of sight—
"Happy Christmas to all, and to all a good night!"

"A Lazy Thought"   *by Eve Merriam*

There go the grown-ups
To the office,
To the store.
Subway rush,
Traffic crush;
Hurry, scurry,
Worry, flurry.
No wonder
Grown ups
Don't grow up
Any more.
It takes a lot
Of slow
To grow.

"Tiptoe"   *by Karla Kuskin*

First line: "Yesterday I skipped all day"

This poem can be found in the following:
Larrick, Nancy. *Piping down the Valleys Wild: Poetry for the Young of All Ages.* Illus. by Ellen Raskin. New York: Bantam Doubleday Dell Books for Young Readers, 1999.
Martin, Bill, and Michael R. Sampson, eds. *The Bill Martin Jr. Big Book of Poetry.* New York: Simon and Schuster Books for Young Readers, 2008.

"First Snow"   *by Marie Louise Allen*

First line: "Snow makes whiteness where it falls"

This poem can be found in the following:

> Arbuthnot, May Hill, and Shelton L. Root, eds. *Time for Poetry: A Representative Collection of Poetry for Children, to Be Used in the Classroom, Home, or Camp; Especially Planned for College Classes in Children's Literature.* Illus. by Arthur Paul. Glenview, IL: Scott, Foresman, 1967.
>
> Austin, Mary C., and Queenie Beatrice Mills. *The Sound of Poetry.* Boston: Allyn and Bacon, 1963.
>
> de Regniers, Beatrice Schenk, ed. *Sing a Song of Popcorn: Every Child's Book of Poems.* Illus. by Marcia Brown. New York: Scholastic, 1988.
>
> Prelutsky, Jack, ed. *The Random House Book of Poetry for Children.* Illus. by Arnold Lobel. New York: Random House, 1983.
>
> Prelutsky, Jack, ed. *Read-Aloud Rhymes for the Very Young.* Illus. by Marc Brown. New York: Knopf, 1986.

"Stop—Go"   *by Dorothy W. Baruch*

Automobiles
In
A
Row
Wait to go
While the signal says:
Stop

Bells ring
Tingaling
Red light's gone;
Green light's on!
Horns blow!
And the row
Starts
To
Go

This poem can be found in the following:

> *Sung under the Silver Umbrella: Poems for Young Children.* Illus. by Dorothy P. Lathrop. New York: Macmillan, 1944.
>
> "Full Text of 'Sung under the Silver Umbrella Poems for Young Children'" at www.archive.org/stream/sungunderthesilv008930mbp/sungunder thesilv008930mbp_djv.txt.

"Christmas Finger Play" —*Anon.*

Here is the wreath that we hang on the door.
Here is the Christmas tree that stands on the floor.
Here is the snow that will cover the town.
Here is the roof that Santa will come down.
Here is the mantle where stockings are hung.
Here is a book from which carols are sung.
Here is a box and inside it is hid
the Jack that pops up when you open the lid.

II. Nursery Rhymes for Choral Reading

Smooth stones from the brook of time,
worn round by constant friction of tongues long silent.
—Andrew Lang, *The Nursery Rhyme Book*

School librarian Katie Blake included the above quote in her original Childread program. It perfectly encapsulates the essence of nursery rhymes. All children deserve to have these rhymes trip off their tongues and become part of their cultural literacy. The following three sets of nursery rhymes are designed to be used with progressively older children. Published nursery-rhyme collections are almost too numerous to mention. Some of my favorites are listed in the bibliography at the end of this section. If an illustrator's name appears next to the nursery rhyme collection, that indicates that it is a recommended illustration to show children when sharing this particular rhyme. The visual interpretations of these nursery rhymes are often lively, quirky, and delightful.

Set 1

1. Peter, Peter pumpkin eater,
   Had a wife and couldn't keep her,
   He put her in a pumpkin shell
   And there he kept her very well.

2. Little Boy Blue, come blow your horn,
   The sheep's in the meadow, the cow's in the corn.
   But where is the boy who looks after the sheep?
   He's under the haystack, fast asleep.

3.   Old Mother Hubbard
     Went to the cupboard,
     To fetch her poor dog a bone;
     When she got there,
     The cupboard was bare
     And so the poor dog had none.

4.   Little Poll Parrot
     Sat in her garret
     Eating toast and tay;
     A little brown mouse
     Jumped into the house,
     And stole it all away.

5.   Betty Botter bought some butter,
     But, she said, the butter's bitter;
     If I put it in my batter
     It will make my batter bitter,

     But a bit of better butter
     Will make my batter better.
     So she bought a bit of butter
     Better than her bitter butter

     And she put it in her batter
     And her batter was not bitter.
     So 'twas better Betty Botter
     Bought a bit of better butter.

6.   There was a little girl
     And she had a little curl
     Right in the middle
     Of her forehead.
     And when she was good
     She was very, very good.
     But when she was bad,
     She was horrid.

7.   Elsie Marley has grown so fine
     She won't get up to feed the swine,
     But lies in bed till eight or nine.
     Lazy Elsie Marley.

8.   Mary, Mary, quite contrary.
     How does your garden grow?

With silver bells and cockleshells,
And pretty maids all in a row.

9. Bow, wow wow!
    Whose dog art thou?
    Little Tommy Tinker's dog.
    Bow, wow, wow!

10. Little Miss Muffet sat on a tuffet
    Eating her curds and whey;
    Along came a spider
    And sat down beside her
    And frightened Miss Muffet away.

11. Little Tommy Tucker
    Sings for his supper.
    What shall he eat?
    White bread and butter.

    How will he cut it
    Without 'ere a knife?
    How can he marry?
    Without 'ere a wife?

12. Barber, barber
    Shave a pig.
    How many hairs
    Will make a wig?
    Four and twenty; That's enough.
    Give the barber a pinch of snuff.

13. Thirty days hath September
    April, June and November.
    February has twenty-eight alone,
    All the rest have thirty-one.
    Except in leap year, that's the time
    When February's days are twenty-nine.

14. What are little boys made of?
    What are little boys made of?
    Snakes and snails and puppy dogs' tails.
    And that's what little boys are made of.

15. This little pig went to market;
    This little pig stayed home;
    This little pig had roast beef;

This little pig had none;
This little pig cried "Wee, wee, wee!"
All the way home.

16. Spring is showery, flowery, bowery;
Summer: hoppy, croppy, poppy;
Autumn: wheezy, sneezy, freezy;
Winter: slippy, drippy, nippy.

17. Rub-a-dub-dub
Three men in a tub,
And who do you think they be?
The butcher, the baker,
The candlestick maker.
And they all jumped out of a rotten potato!
Turn them out, knaves all three.

18. Oh where, oh where has my little dog gone?
Oh where, oh where can he be?
With his ears cut short and his tail cut long,
Oh where, oh where is he?

19. Mary had a little lamb
Its fleece was white as snow
And everywhere that Mary went
The lamb was sure to go.

It followed her to school one day
That was against the rule;
It made the children laugh and play
To see a lamb at school.

And so the teacher turned it out
But still it lingered near.
And waited patiently about
Till Mary did appear.

"Why does the lamb love Mary so?"
The eager children cry.
"Why, Mary loves the lamb, you know,"
The teacher did reply.

20. There was a crooked man
And he went a crooked mile;
He found a crooked sixpence
Against a crooked stile;

He bought a crooked cat,
Which caught a crooked mouse;
And they all lived together
In a little crooked house.

21. Jack and Jill
Went up the hill,
To fetch a pail of water;
Jack fell down,
And broke his crown,
And Jill came tumbling after.

22. Rock-a-bye baby,
On the tree top,
When the wind blows,
The cradle will rock;

When the bough breaks,
The cradle will fall,
And down will come baby,
Cradle and all.

23. Bye, baby Bunting
Daddy's gone a-hunting
Gone to get a rabbit skin
To wrap the baby Bunting in.

24. Pussy cat, pussy cat
Where have you been?
I've been to London
To visit the queen.
Pussy cat, pussy cat
What did you there?
I frightened a little mouse
Under her chair.

25. Diddle, diddle dumpling, my son John,
Went to bed with his trousers on;
One shoe off, and one shoe on,
Diddle, diddle dumpling, my son John.

26. Three little kittens
They lost their mittens
And they began to cry,
Oh mother dear, we sadly fear
Our mittens we have lost.

What! Lost your mittens,
You naughty kittens!
Then you shall have no pie.
Mee-ow
Mee-ow
Mee-ow
No, you shall have no pie.

27. Old King Cole
Was a merry old soul,
And a merry old soul was he;
He called for his pipe,
And he called for his bowl,
And he called for his fiddlers three.

Every fiddler, he had a fiddle,
And a very fine fiddle had he;
Oh, there's none so rare,
As can compare
With King Cole and his fiddlers three.

28. There was an old woman who lived in a shoe,
She had so many children, she didn't know what to do;
She gave them some broth without any bread,
And whipped them all soundly and put them to bed.

29. Cobbler, cobbler, mend my shoe,
Get it done by half-past two.
Half-past two is far too late,
Get it done by half-past eight.

30. Charley Barley butter and eggs,
Sold his wife for three duck eggs.
When the ducks began to lay
Charley Barley flew away.

31. Goosey, goosey, gander.
Where do you wander?
Upstairs and downstairs
And in my lady's chamber.

There I met an old man
Who would not say his prayers,
I took him by the left leg
And threw him down the stairs.

32. Wee Willie Winkie
Runs through the town.
Upstairs, downstairs
In his nightgown.

Rapping at the window
Crying through the lock.
"Are all the children all in bed?
For now it's eight o'clock."

33. Snip, snap, snout.
Our tale is out!

Set 2
---

1. Fee, fie, fo, fum!
I smell the blood of an Englishman.
Be he alive or be he dead,
I'll grind his bones to make my bread.

2. Tom, Tom the piper's son,
Stole a pig and away he run!
The pig was eat, and Tom was beat,
And Tom went roaring down the street!

3. Humpty Dumpty sat on a wall,
Humpty Dumpty had a great fall.
All the king's horses
And all the king's men,
Couldn't put Humpty Dumpty together again.

4. Ugly babies
Make pretty ladies.

5. Tweedledum and Tweedledee
Resolved to have a battle,
For Tweedledum said Tweedledee
Had spoiled his nice new rattle.

Just then flew by a monstrous crow,
As big as a tar barrel,
Which frightened both the heroes so,
They quite forgot their quarrel.

6. Two legs sat upon three legs
   With one leg in his lap;
   In comes four legs
   And runs away with one leg.
   Up jumps two legs,
   Catches up three legs,
   Throws it after four legs,
   And makes him bring back one leg.
   Answer: One leg is a leg of mutton; two legs, a man; three legs,
   a stool; four legs, a dog.

7. Here I am, Little Jumping Joan
   When nobody's with me,
   I'm all alone.

8. An apple a day
   Keeps the doctor away.

9. Hickory, dickory, dock.
   The mouse ran up the clock.
   The clock struck one,
   And down he ran,
   Hickory, dickory, dock.

10. There was a crooked man, and he went a crooked mile,
    He found a crooked sixpence against a crooked stile;
    He bought a crooked cat, which caught a crooked mouse,
    And they all lived together in a crooked little house.

11. To scratch where it itches
    Is better than fine clothes or riches.

12. Little Miss Muffet
    Sat on a tuffet,
    Eating her curds and whey;
    Along came a spider
    And sat down beside her
    And frightened Miss Muffet away.

13. Dingty diddledy
    My mammy's maid,
    She stole oranges,
    I am afraid;

    Some in her pocket,
    Some in her sleeve,

She stole oranges,
I do believe.

14. Four stiff-standers
    Four dilly-danders
    Two lookers, two crookers
    And a wig-wag.

15. The grand old Duke of York
    He had ten thousand men;
    He marched them up to the top of the hill,
    And he marched them down again.

    And when they were up, they were up.
    And when they were down, they were down.
    And when they were only halfway up,
    They were neither up nor down.

16. There was a man in our town,
    And he was wondrous wise,
    He jumped into a quickset hedge,
    And scratched out both his eyes.

    And when he saw his eyes were out,
    With all his might and main
    He jumped into another hedge,
    And scratched them in again.

17. Granfa' Grig had a pig,
    In a field of clover;
    Piggie dies, Granfa cried,
    And all the fun was over.
    (Use Wallace Tripp's illustration to share this rhyme.)

18. Hey! Diddle, diddle,
    The cat and the fiddle
    The cow jumped over the moon;
    The little dog laugh'd
    To see such sport
    And the dish ran away with the spoon.
    (Use Arthur Rackham's illustration to share this rhyme.)

19. The captain was a duck,
    With a packet on his back;
    And when the ship began to move,
    The captain said, "Quack! Quack!"

20. There was an old woman
Lived under a hill,
And if she's not gone
She lives there still.

21. Three wise men of Gotham
Went to sea in a bowl;
And if the bowl had been stronger,
My song would have been longer.

22. Pussy-cat, pussy-cat
Where have you been?
I've been to London
To visit the queen.

Pussy-cat, pussy-cat
What did you there?
I frighten'd a little mouse
Under the chair.

23. Little Bo-Peep has lost her sheep,
And can't tell where to find them;
Leave them alone, and they'll come home,
Wagging their tails behind them.

24. Little Tommy Tucker
Sings for his supper.
What shall he eat?
White bread and butter.

How will he cut it
Without 'ere a knife?
How can he marry
Without 'ere a wife?

25. "Where are you going to, my pretty maid?"
"I'm going a-milking, sir," she said.
"May I go with you, my pretty maid?"
"Yes, if you please, kind sir," she said.

"What is your father, my pretty maid?"
"My father's a farmer, sir," she said.
"What is your fortune, my pretty maid?"
"My face is my fortune, sir," she said.

"Then I can't marry you, my pretty maid."
"Nobody asked you, sir!" she said.

26. Baa, baa, black sheep
Have you any wool?
Yes sir, yes sir
Three bags full:
One for my master, and one for my dame,
But none for the little boy who cries in the lane.

27. Intery, mintery, cutery corn,
Apple seed and apple thorn;
Wine, brier, limber lock,
Three geese in a flock,
One flew east, one flew west,
And one flew over the cuckoo's nest.

28. Doctor Foster went to Glo'ster
In a shower of rain.
He stepped in a puddle,
Up to his middle,
And never went there again.

29. Peter White
Will ne'er go right
Would you know
The reason why?
He follows his nose
Wherever he goes,
And that stands
All awry.

30. The giant Jim
Great giant grim
Wears a hat
Without a brim.
Weighs a ton
And wears a blouse,
And trembles when
He meets a mouse.

31. Little Jack Horner
Sat in a corner,
Eating a Christmas pie;
He put in his thumb,
And pulled out a plum,
And said, "What a good boy am I!"

32. Georgie Porgie, pudding and pie,
Kissed the girls and made them cry;
When the boys came out to play,
Georgie Porgie ran away.

33. Jack Sprat could eat no fat,
His wife could eat no lean:
And so, betwixt the both, you see,
They licked the platter clean.

34. Little Boy Blue, come blow your horn
The sheep's in the meadow, the cow's in the corn.
Where is the boy that looks after the sheep?
He's under the haystack fast asleep!

Set 3

1. Higgledy, piggledy, my black hen
She lays eggs for gentlemen;
Gentlemen come every day
To see what my black hen doth lay,
Sometimes nine, and sometimes ten,
Higgledy, piggledy, my black hen!
*(Use Alice and Martin Provensen's or Wallace Tripp's illustration
to share this rhyme.)*

2. Higgledy, piggledy, pop!
The dog has eaten the mop;
The pig's in a hurry,
The cat's in a flurry
Higgledy, piggledy, pop!
(Use Wallace Tripp's illustration to share this rhyme.)

3. Handy pandy, Jack-a-Dandy,
Loves plum cake and sugar candy.
He bought some at the grocer's shop,
And out he came, hop, hop, hop!

4. Brow brinky,
Eye winky,
Chin choppy,
Cheek cherry,
Mouth merry.

5. Tickly, tickly
   On your knee;
   If you laugh
   You don't love me.

6. Little Jack Horner,
   Sat in a corner,
   Eating a Christmas pie;
   He put in his thumb,
   And pulled out a plum,
   And said, "What a good boy am I!"

7. Jack be nimble,
   Jack be quick,
   Jack jump over
   The candlestick.

8. Little Nancy Etticoat
   In a white petticoat,
   And a red nose.
   The longer she stands
   The shorter she grows.
   (This riddle describes a candle.)

9. Dickery, dickery dare,
   The pig flew up in the air;
   The man in brown
   Soon brought him down,
   Dickery, dickery dare.

10. Mix a pancake,
    Stir a pancake,
    Pop it in the pan;
    Toss the pancake—
    Catch it if you can.

11. Daffadowndilly
    Has come up to town
    In a yellow petticoat
    And a green gown.

12. Little Jack Sprat
    Once had a pig;
    It was not very little,
    Nor yet very big,

It was not very lean,
It was not very fat—
"It's a good pig to grunt,"
Said Little Jack Sprat.

13. To market, to market, to buy a fat pig.
Home again, home again, jiggety-jig.
To market, to market, to buy a fat hog,
Home again, home again, jiggety-jog.

14. There once were two cats of Kilkenny,
Each thought there was one cat too many.
So they fought and they fit,
And they scratched and they bit,
Till, excepting their nails,
And the tips of their tails
Instead of two cats, there weren't any.
(Use James Marshall's illustration to share this rhyme.)

15. A wise old owl lived in an oak;
The more he saw, the less he spoke;
The less he spoke, the more he heard.
Why aren't we all like that wise old bird?
(Use Wallace Tripp's illustration to share this rhyme.)

16. Pease-porridge hot,
Pease-porridge cold,
Pease-porridge in the pot,
Nine days old.
Some like it hot,
Some like it cold,
Some like it in the pot,
Nine days old.

17. Peter Piper picked a peck of pickled peppers;
A peck of pickled peppers Peter Piper picked.
If Peter Piper picked a peck of pickled peppers,
Where's the peck of pickled peppers Peter Piper picked?

18. Little Tommy Tittlemouse
Lived in a little house;
He caught fishes
In other men's ditches.
(Use James Marshall's illustration to share this rhyme.)

19. Simple Simon met a pieman, going to the fair;
Says Simple Simon to the pieman, "Let me taste your ware."
Says the pieman to Simple Simon, "Show me first your penny."
Says Simple Simon to the pieman, "Indeed I have not any."
(Use Alice and Martin Provensen's illustration to share this rhyme.)

20. Polly put the kettle on,
Polly put the kettle on,
Polly put the kettle on,
We'll all have tea.

Sukey take it off again,
Sukey take it off again,
Sukey take it off again,
They've all gone away.
(Use Wallace Tripp's illustration to share this rhyme.)

21. Solomon Grundy,
Born on a Monday
Christened on Tuesday
Married on Wednesday
Took ill on Thursday
Worse on Friday
Died on Saturday
Buried on Sunday
This is the end of Solomon Grundy.
(Use James Marshall's illustration to share this rhyme.)

22. Ride a cock-horse to Coventry Cross, *[or "Banbury Town"]*
To see a fine lady upon a white horse;
Rings on her fingers and bells on her toes,
She shall have music wherever she goes.
(Use Wallace Tripp's illustration to share this rhyme.)

23. There was an old woman tossed in a blanket
Seventeen times as high as the moon;
What she did there, I cannot tell you,
But in her hand she carried a broom.

"Old woman, old woman, old woman," said I.
"Whither, oh whither, oh whither so high?"
"To sweep the cobwebs from the sky,
And I'll be with you by and by."
(Use Wallace Tripp's illustration to share this rhyme.)

24. One, two, three, four, five
I caught a fish alive
"Why did you let them go?"
"Because they bit my finger so."
"Which finger did they bite?"
"The little finger on the right."

25. 1, 2 ; Buckle my shoe;
3, 4; Shut the door;
5, 6; Pick up sticks;
7, 8; Lay them straight;

9, 10; A big fat hen;
11, 12; Dig and delve;
13, 14; Maids are courting;
15, 16; Maids in the kitchen;

17, 18; Maids are waiting;
19, 20; My plate's empty.
(Use Feodor Rojankovsky's illustration to share this rhyme.)

26. I love little pussy,
Her coat is so warm,
And if I don't hurt her
She'll do me no harm.
So I'll not pull her tail,
Nor drive her away,
But pussy and I
Very gently will play.
She shall sit by my side,
And I'll give her some food;
And pussy will love me
Because I am good.

27. Cross patch,
Draw the latch,
Sit by the fire and spin;
Take a cup
And drink it up,
And call your neighbors in.
(Use Feodor Rojankovsky's illustration to share this rhyme.)

28. Hush-a-by, baby
Daddy is near;

Mamma is a lady,
And that's very clear.

29. "Old woman, old woman
Shall we go a-shearing?"
"Speak a little louder, sir,
I am very thick of hearing."

"Old woman, old woman,
Shall I love you dearly?"
"Thank you kind sir,
I hear you very clearly."

30. Curly locks! Curly locks!
Wilt thou be mine?
Thou shalt not wash dishes, nor yet feed the swine,
But sit on the cushion and sew a fine seam,
And feed upon strawberries, sugar and cream!

31. For want of a nail, the shoe was lost,
For want of a shoe, the horse was lost,
For want of a horse, the rider was lost,
For want of a rider, the message was lost,
For want of a message, the battle was lost,
For the want of a battle, the kingdom was lost,
And all for the want of a horseshoe nail.

32. Hot cross buns!
Hot cross buns!
One a penny, two a penny,
Hot cross buns!

If your daughters do not like them
Give them to your sons!
But if you haven't any of these pretty little elves
You cannot do better than to eat them yourselves.
—*Old London street cry*

33. As I was going to St. Ives,
I met a man with seven wives;
Each wife had seven sacks,
Each sack had seven cats,
Each cat had seven kits;

Kits, cats, sacks, and wives,
How many were going to St. Ives?

34. O, that I were where I would be,
Then would I be where I am not;
But where I am there I must be,
And where I would be I cannot.

35. How many miles to Babylon?
Three score and ten.
Can I get there by candlelight?
Yes, and back again.
If your heels are nimble and light,
You may get there by candlelight.

36. I've got a rocket
In my pocket;
I cannot stop to play.
Away it goes!
I've burned my toes.
It's Independence Day.

37. A diller, a dollar
A ten o'clock scholar,
What makes you come so soon?
You used to come at ten o'clock
But now you come at noon.
(Use Wallace Tripp's illustration to share this rhyme.)

38. Sing a song of sixpence,
A pocket full of rye;
Four and twenty blackbirds
Baked in a pie.

When the pie was opened
The birds began to sing;
Wasn't that a dainty dish
To set before the king?

The king was in his counting-house
Counting out his money;
The queen was in the parlor
Eating bread and honey.

The maid was in the garden
Hanging out the clothes,
When down came a blackbird
And snapped off her nose.
(Use Wallace Tripp's illustration to share this rhyme.)

39. Monday's child is fair of face,
Tuesday's child is full of grace,
Wednesday's child is full of woe,
Thursday's child has far to go,

Friday's child is loving and giving,
Saturday's child works hard for a living.
But the child who is born on the Sabbath day
Is bonny and blithe and good and gay.
(Use Feodor Rojankovsky's illustration to share this rhyme.)

40. Twinkle, twinkle, little star,
How I wonder what you are!
Up above the world so high,
Like a diamond in the sky.

As your bright and tiny spark,
Lights the traveler in the dark—
Though I know not what you are,
Twinkle, twinkle, little star.

41. Lady bird, lady bird, fly away home:
Your house is on fire, your children are gone—
All but one and her name is Ann,
And she crept under the pudding-pan.
(Use Arthur Rackham's illustration to share this rhyme.)

42. It's raining, it's pouring,
The old man is snoring;
He got into bed
And bumped his head
And wouldn't get up in the morning.

43. One misty, moisty morning,
When cloudy was the weather,
I chanced to meet an old man
Clothed all in leather;

He began to compliment,
And I began to grin—
"How do you do,"
And "How do you do,"
And "How do you do," again!
(Use Feodor Rojankovsky's illustration to share this rhyme.)

44. Cocks crow in the morn
To tell us to rise,
For he who lies late
Will never be wise;

For early to bed and early to rise,
Makes a man healthy, wealthy and wise.
He that would thrive,
Must rise at five;

He that has thriven
May lie till seven;
And he that will never thrive
May lie till eleven.

45. Wear you a hat or wear you a crown,
All that goes up must surely come down.
(Use Wallace Tripp's illustration to share this rhyme.)

46. One thing at a time
And that done well,
Is a very good rule,
As many can tell.
(Use Wallace Tripps's illustration to share this rhyme.)

47. Bow-wow, says the dog;
Mew-mew, says the cat;
Grunt-grunt, goes the hog;
And squeak goes the rat.

Tu-whu, says the owl;
Caw-caw, says the crow;
Quack-quack, says the duck;
And what sparrows say you know.

So, with sparrows, and owls,
With rats, and with dogs,
With ducks, and with crows,
With cats, and with hogs,

A fine song I have made,
To please you, my dear;
And if it's well sung,
'Twill be charming to hear.
(Children can make all of the animal sounds at once
after the poem is recited.)

48. Snip, snap, snout
Our tale is out!

49. Rain, rain go away,
Come again another day;
Little Johnny wants to play.
(Use Feodor Rojankovsky's illustration to share this rhyme.)

50. Christmas is coming, the geese are getting fat,
Please to put a penny in an old man's hat;
If you haven't got a penny a ha'penny will do,
If you haven't got a ha'penny, God bless you.
(Use Feodor Rojankovsky's illustration to share this rhyme.)

Nursery Rhyme Bibliography

Chorao, Kay. *The Baby's Bedtime Book.* New York: Dutton, 1984.

Chorao, Kay. *The Baby's Good Morning Book.* New York: Dutton, 1986.

Chorao, Kay. *The Baby's Lap Book.* New York: Dutton, 1977.

Chorao, Kay. *Kay Chorao's Big Book for Babies.* New York: Barnes and Noble, 1998.

Lobel, Arnold, illus. *The Arnold Lobel Book of Mother Goose.* New York: Knopf, 1997.

Marshall, James. *Pocketful of Nonsense.* New York: Artists and Writers Guild, 1993.

Provensen, Alice, and Martin Provensen, illus. *The Mother Goose Book.* New York: Random House, 1976.

Rojankovsky, Feodor, illus. *The Tall Book of Mother Goose.* New York: Harper and Bros., 1942.

Tudor, Tasha, illus. *Mother Goose.* New York: Henry Z. Walck, 1972.

Tripp, Wallace, ed. *Granfa' Grig Had a Pig: And Other Rhymes without Reason.* Boston: Little, Brown, 1976.

III. Folktales and Fairy Stories

Individual Fairy Tales

Baba Yaga (Russia)

Kimmel, Eric A. *Baba Yaga: A Russian Folktale.* Illus. by Megan Lloyd. New York: Holiday House, 1991.

Waddell, Martin. *Baba Yaga.* Illus. by David Lopez. London: Franklin Watts, 2009.

Yolen, Jane. *Baba Yaga.* Illus. by Vladimir Vasilevich Vagin. New York: HarperCollins, 2002.

Beauty and the Beast

Brett, Jan. *Beauty and the Beast.* New York: Clarion, 1989.

Eilenberg, Max. *Beauty and the Beast.* Illus. by Angela Barrett. Cambridge, MA: Candlewick, 2006.

Mayer, Marianna, and Mercer Mayer, author and illus. *Beauty and the Beast.* New York: Four Winds, 1978.

Willard, Nancy. *Beauty and the Beast.* Illus. by Barry Moser. San Diego: Harcourt Brace Jovanovich, 1992.

The Bremen Town Musicians

Stevens, Janet, author and illus. *The Bremen Town Musicians.* New York: Holiday House, 1992.

Wildsmith, Brian, author and illus. *The Bremen Town Musicians.* New York: Star Bright, 2012.

Cinderella

Galdone, Paul, illus. *Cinderella.* New York: McGraw-Hill, 1978.

Perrault, Charles. *Cinderella.* Illus. by Diane Goode. New York: Knopf, 1988.

The Gingerbread Boy

Egielski, Richard, author and illus. *The Gingerbread Boy.* New York: Laura Geringer, 1997.

Galdone, Paul, illus. *The Gingerbread Boy.* New York: Seabury, 1975.

Ziefert, Harriet. *The Gingerbread Boy.* Illus. by Emily Bolam. New York: Viking, 1995.

Hansel and Gretel

Lesser, Rika, Wilhelm Grimm, and Jacob Grimm. *Hansel and Gretel.* Illus. by Paul O. Zelinsky. New York: Dodd, Mead and Company, 1984.

Marshall, James. *Hansel and Gretel.* New York: Dial Books for Young Readers, 1990.

Montresor, Beni, illus. *Hansel and Gretel.* New York: Atheneum Books for Young Readers, 2001.

Rylant, Cynthia. *Hansel and Gretel.* Illus. by Jen Corace. New York: Hyperion Books for Children, 2008.

Henny Penny

French, Vivian. *Henny Penny.* Illus. by Sophie Windham. New York: Bloomsbury Children's Books, 2006.

Galdone, Paul, illus. *Henny Penny.* New York: Seabury, 1968.

The House That Jack Built

Caldecott, Randolph. *The House That Jack Built.* New York: Avenel, 1975.

Galdone, Paul, illus. *The House That Jack Built.* New York: Whittlesey House, 1961.

Stow, Jenny. *The House That Jack Built.* New York: Dial Books for Young Readers, 1992.

Winter, Jeanette, author and illus. *The House That Jack Built.* New York: Dial Books for Young Readers, 2000.

Little Red Riding Hood

Hyman, Trina Schart, author and illus., Jacob Grimm, and Wilhelm Grimm. *Little Red Riding Hood.* New York: Holiday House, 1983.

Pinkney, Jerry, Jacob Grimm, and Wilhelm Grimm. *Little Red Riding Hood.* New York: Little, Brown, 2007.

Puss in Boots

Cauley, Lorinda Bryan, Michael Farmer, and Charles Perrault. *Puss in Boots.* San Diego: Harcourt Brace Jovanovich, 1986.

Galdone, Paul, illus. *Puss in Boots.* New York: Seabury, 1976.

Perrault, Charles, and Malcolm Arthur. *Puss in Boots.* Illus. by Fred Marcellino. New York: Farrar, Straus and Giroux, 1990.

Pinkney, Jerry. *Puss in Boots.* New York: Dial Books for Young Readers, 2012.

Rapunzel

Zelinsky, Paul O., Amy Beniker, and John Stevens. *Rapunzel.* New York: Dutton Children's Books, 1997.

Rumplestiltskin

Zelinsky, Paul O., illus. *Rumplestiltskin.* New York: Dutton, 1986.

Seven Ravens

Hoffmann, Felix, Jacob Grimm, Wilhelm Grimm, and Fritz Eichenberg. *The Seven Ravens.* New York: Harcourt, Brace and World, 1963.

Wildsmith, Brian, author and illus. *The Seven Ravens.* Oxford: Oxford University Press, 1999.

The Shoemaker and the Elves

Grimm, Jacob, and Wilhelm Grimm. *The Shoemaker and the Elves.* Illus. by Adrienne Adams. New York: Scribner, 1960.

Plume, Ilse. *The Shoemaker and the Elves.* San Diego: Harcourt Brace Jovanovich, 1991.

Sleeping Beauty

Hyman, Trina Schart, and Jacob Grimm. *The Sleeping Beauty.* Boston: Little, Brown, 1977.

Mayer, Mercer. *The Sleeping Beauty.* New York: Macmillan, 1984.

Snow White

Grimm, Jacob, and Wilhelm Grimm. *Snow White and Rose Red.* Illus. by Adrienne Adams. New York: Scribner, 1964.

Grimm, Jacob, Wilhelm Grimm, Randall Jarrell, and Atha Tehon. *Snow White and the Seven Dwarfs.* Illus. by Nancy Ekholm Burkert. New York: Farrar, Straus and Giroux, 1972.

Grimm, Jacob, Wilhelm Grimm, and Errol Le Cain. *Thorn Rose.* Scarsdale, NY: Bradbury, 1977.

The Three Bears

Barton, Byron, author and illus. *The Three Bears.* New York: HarperCollins, 1991.

Galdone, Paul, illus. *The Three Bears.* New York: Seabury, 1972.

Rojankovsky, Feodor, illus. *The Three Bears.* New York: Golden, 1948.

The Three Billy Goats Gruff

Asbjørnsen, Peter Christen. *The Three Billy Goats Gruff*. New York: Holiday House, 1993.

Stevens, Janet. *The Three Billy Goats Gruff*. San Diego: Harcourt Brace Jovanovich, 1987.

The Three Little Pigs

Galdone, Paul, illus. *The Three Little Pigs*. New York: Houghton Mifflin/ Clarion, 1970.

Kellogg, Steven. *The Three Little Pigs*. New York: Morrow Junior Books, 1997.

Marshall, James. *The Three Little Pigs*. New York: Dial Books for Young Readers, 1989.

The Ugly Duckling (Danish)

Crossley-Holland, Kevin, and Hans Christian Andersen. *The Ugly Duckling*. Illus. by Meilo So. New York: Alfred Knopf, 2001.

Andersen, Hans Christian. *The Ugly Duckling*. Illus. by Jerry Pinkney. New York: Morrow Junior Books, 1999.

Classic Picture-Book Folktale Adaptations

Aardema, Verna, Warren Wallerstein, and Atha Tehon. *Why Mosquitoes Buzz in People's Ears: A West African Tale*. Illus. by Leo Dillon and Diane Dillon. New York: Dial, 1975.

Bang, Molly. *Wiley and the Hairy Man: Adapted from an American Folktale*. New York: Macmillan, 1976. (American)

Bowden, Joan Chase. *Why the Tides Ebb and Flow*. Illus. by Marc Brown. Boston: Houghton Mifflin, 1979.

Brown, Marcia, author and illus. *Dick Whittington and His Cat*. New York: Scribner, 1950. (English)

Brown, Marcia, author and illus. *Once a Mouse: A Fable Cut in Wood*. New York: Scribner, 1961.

Cauley, Lorinda Bryan. *The Cock, the Mouse, and the Little Red Hen*. New York: Putnam, 1982.

Chafetz, Henry, and Ronni Solbert. *The Legend of Befana*. Boston: Houghton Mifflin, 1958.

dePaola, Tomie. *Big Anthony and the Magic Ring: Story and Pictures*. New York: Harcourt Brace Jovanovich, 1979.

dePaola, Tomie. *Strega Nona: An Old Tale*. Englewood Cliffs, NJ: Prentice-Hall, 1975.

Elkin, Benjamin. *Six Foolish Fishermen.* Illus. by Katherine Evans. Eau Claire, WI: Hale, 1962.

Emberley, Barbara. *Drummer Hoff.* Illus. by Ed Emberley. Englewood Cliffs, NJ: Prentice-Hall, 1967.

Galdone, Paul, illus. *The Old Woman and Her Pig.* New York: McGraw-Hill, 1960.

Grimm, Jacob, and Wilhelm Grimm. *The Golden Goose.* Illus. by Uri Shulevitz. New York: Farrar, Straus and Giroux, 1995.

Grimm, Jacob, and Wilhelm Grimm. *Tom Thumb.* Illus. by Felix Hoffmann. New York: Atheneum, 1973.

Gurvin, Abe, author and illus. *The Husband Who Was to Mind the House.* New York: Young Readers, 1968.

Haley, Gail E., author and illus. *A Story, a Story: An African Tale.* New York: Atheneum, 1970.

Haviland, Virginia. "The Good Housewife and Her Night Labors." In *Favorite Fairy Tales Told in Scotland.* Illus. by Adrienne Adams. Boston: Little, Brown, 1963.

Hodges, Margaret. *Dick Whittington and His Cat.* Illus. by Mélisande Potter. New York: Holiday House, 2006. (English)

Huber, Miriam Blanton. *Mr. Vinegar.* Nisbet, 1952.

Jacobs, Joseph. *King of the Cats: A Ghost Story.* Illus. by Paul Galdone. New York: Houghton Mifflin/Clarion, 1980.

Jacobs, Joseph. *The Three Sillies.* Illus. by Paul Galdone. New York: Clarion, 1981.

Jacobs, Joseph. *The Three Sillies.* Illus. by Steven Kellogg. Cambridge, MA: Candlewick, 1999.

Jaquith, Priscilla, Duncan Emrich, and Albert Henry Stoddard. *Bo Rabbit Smart for True: Folktales from the Gullah.* Illus. by Ed Young. New York: Philomel, 1981.

Kellogg, Steven, author and illus. *Jack and the Beanstalk.* New York: Morrow Junior Books, 1991.

Kent, Jack. *The Fat Cat: A Danish Folktale.* New York: Parent's Magazine, 1971

Kimmel, Eric A. *Anansi and the Moss-covered Rock.* Illus. by Janet Stevens. New York: Holiday House, 1988.

Kimmel, Eric A. *The Old Woman and Her Pig.* Illus. by Giora Carmi. New York: Holiday House, 1992.

King-Smith, Dick. *The Golden Goose.* Illus. by Ann Kronheimer. New York: Knopf, 2005.

Lester, Julius. *John Henry.* Illus. by Jerry Pinkney. New York: Dial, 1994.

McDermott, Gerald. *Anansi the Spider: A Tale from the Ashanti.* New York: Holt, Rinehart and Winston, 1972.

McDermott, Gerald. *Arrow to the Sun: A Pueblo Indian Tale.* New York: Viking, 1974.

Mosel, Arlene. *Tikki Tikki Tembo.* Illus. by Blair Lent. New York: Holt, Rinehart and Winston, 1968.

Ormerod, Jan. *The Frog Prince.* New York: Lothrop, Lee and Shepard, 1990.

Percy, Graham. *The Cock, the Mouse, and the Little Red Hen: A Traditional Tale.* Cambridge, MA: Candlewick, 1992.

Richardson, Frederick. *Great Children's Stories: A Treasured Collection.* Franklin, TN: Dalmatian, 2000.

Robbins, Ruth. *Baboushka and the Three Kings.* Illus. by Nicolas Sidjakov. Berkeley: Parnassus, 1960.

Root, Betty. *Travels of a Fox.* Illus. by Eric Kincaid. London: Macdonald Educational, 1976.

Rose, Anne K. *As Right as Right Can Be.* Illus. by Arnold Lobel. New York: Dial, 1976.

San Souci, Robert D. *Six Foolish Fishermen.* Illus. by Doug Kennedy. New York: Hyperion Books for Children, 2000.

Shannon, George. *Bean Boy.* Illus. by Peter Sís. New York: Greenwillow, 1984.

Sierra, Judy. *Wiley and the Hairy Man.* Illus. by Brian Pinkney. New York: Lodestar, 1996.

Sleator, William. *The Angry Moon.* Illus. by Blair Lent. Boston: Little, Brown, 1970.

Steel, Flora Annie Webster. *Tattercoats: An Old English Tale.* Illus. by Diane Goode. Scarsdale, NY: Bradbury, 1976.

Tarcov, Edith. *The Frog Prince.* Illus. by James Marshall. New York: Scholastic, 1993.

The Travels of a Fox: A British Folk Tale. Illus. by TreeGardner. Glenview, IL: Scott, Foresman, 1971.

Watson, Richard Jesse. *Tom Thumb.* San Diego: Harcourt Brace Jovanovich, 1989.

IV. Fables

Introducing Fables

Did you ever pull a joke on your friends by yelling. "Help" so that everyone ran to see what was the matter with you, and then you said, "Only fooling"? That is called "crying wolf." Have you heard the saying, "Slow and steady wins the race?" Well, you might not have known it, but these sayings go back a long time, clear to ancient Greece. It was there that a man named Aesop told stories about animals who talked. These stories are called fables. You can easily tell a fable because there is always a moral: a short sentence that tells the lesson of the story at the end of each fable.

Here are the names of some of Aesop's most famous fables. Perhaps you have already heard of some of these:

"The Boy Who Cried Wolf"
"The Fox and the Grapes"
"The Tortoise and the Hare"
"The Lion and the Mouse"
"The Dog and his Shadow."

In the library, you will find Aesop's fables in the 398s.

New fables have been written by many authors, including Arnold Lobel. His book *Fables* is full of crazy characters, like an alligator who stays in his bed because he likes the wallpaper. There is a hippopotamus who eats too much and ends up stuck under a restaurant table. There is a kangaroo family who like to throw spitwads across the table and set off firecrackers in the bathroom! And there is a mouse who endures a long and dangerous journey to the seashore.

Here are some great books with fables:

Aesop, and Jerry Pinkney. *Aesop's Fables.* New York: SeaStar, 2000.
Lobel, Arnold, author and illus. *Fables.* New York: Harper and Row, 1980.
Pinkney, Jerry. *The Tortoise and the Hare.* New York: Little Brown and
    Books for Young Readers, 2013.
Pinkney, Jerry, and Aesop. *The Lion & the Mouse.* New York: Little Brown
    and Books for Young Readers, 2009.
Scieszka, Jon. *Squids Will Be Squids: Fresh Morals, Beastly Fables.* Illus. by
    Lane Smith. New York: Viking, 1998.
Stevens, Janet, and Aesop. *The Tortoise and the Hare: An Aesop Fable.* New
    York: Holiday House, 1984.

V. Greek Mythology

Introducing Greek Mythology

Mythology can be effectively introduced to children as early as age six or seven. My first introduction to mythology was in the second grade through the final books in the Programmed Reading series, originally published by Scott Foresman and now available through Phoenix Learning Resources. Programmed Reading books 22 and 23 include a number of Greek myths. These books are available at www.phoenixlearningresources.com/programmed_reading-c-list.aspx.

The bottom line is that children should know the Greek myths in their original form long before they discover Percy Jackson.

The following titles introduce Greek myths and list of myths that children ought to know, with some recommended books including these stories.

Collections of Greek Myths

D'Aulaire, Ingri, and Edgar Parin D'Aulaire. *Ingri and Edgar Parin D'Aulaire's Book of Greek Myths.* Garden City, NY: Doubleday, 1962.

Vinge, Joan D. *The Random House Book of Greek Myths.* Illus. by Oren Sherman. New York: Random House, 1999.

Specific Greek Myths to Introduce

The creation of life

Titans and Cyclops

The reign of Cronus

The War of the Titans

Greek Gods family tree

The Three Great Gods

Jupiter

Neptune

Pluto

Mount Olympus

The creation of humans

Atlas, Prometheus, and Epimetheus/the Three Fates

Prometheus brings fire and is chained to a rock in punishment

Pandora

Burleigh, Robert. *Pandora.* Illus. by Raúl Colón. San Diego: Silver Whistle, 2002.

The story of Io

Juno, Argus, and Mercury
The birth of Mercury
Vulcan's story
Venus
Cupid
Minerva
Ceres and Proserpine
Mars
Diana and the giant brothers
The story of Phaeton
Two tales of King Midas
Craft, Charlotte. *King Midas and the Golden Touch.* Illus. by Kinuko Craft. New York: Morrow, 1999.
Demi. *King Midas: The Golden Touch.* New York: Margaret K. McElderry, 2002.
Philip, Neil. *King Midas.* Illus. by Isabelle Brent. Boston: Little, Brown, 1994.
Stewig, John W., and Omar Rayyan. *King Midas: A Golden Tale.* New York: Holiday House, 1999.
The golden touch
Pan (musical contest between Pan and Apollo)
Arachne
Hovey, Kate. *Arachne Speaks.* Illus. by Blair Drawson. New York: Margaret K. McElderry, 2000.
Atalanta
Fontes, Justine, and Ron Fontes. *Atalanta: The Race against Destiny; A Greek Myth.* Illus. by Thomas Yeates. Minneapolis, MN: Graphic Universe, 2007. (This is a graphic novel.)
Perseus
The birth of Perseus
Minerva and Mercury
The Gray sisters
Perseus and Medusa
Hoena, B. A. *Perseus and Medusa.* Illus. by Daniel Pérez. Minneapolis, MN: Stone Arch, 2009. (This is a graphic novel.)
Andromeda and the sea monster
The return to Greece
Hercules

Hercules

Stories of Hercules have been retold in these books:

Burleigh, Robert. *Hercules*. Illus. by Raúl Colón. San Diego: Silver Whistle, 1999.

Evslin, Bernard. *Hercules*. Illus. by Joseph A. Smith. New York: Morrow, 1984.

McCaughrean, Geraldine. *Hercules*. Chicago: Cricket, 2005.

When introducing Hercules and his twelve labors,
include the following elements:

The birth of Hercules

Juno's plan fails

The education of Hercules—music, reciting poetry, wrestling, driving

The end of the music lessons

The young hero

The Oracle at Delphi

The message

The First Labor—Nemean Lion

The Second Labor—Hydra

The Third Labor—wild stag

The Fourth Labor—wild boar

The Fifth Labor—rid lake of terrible birds

The Sixth Labor—clean Augeas' stables

The Seventh Labor—bring back fire-breathing white bull Neptune had given to King Minos

The Eight Labor—herd of wild mares belonging to King Diomedes

The Ninth Labor—jeweled belt of the Amazon Queen

The Tenth Labor—the Red Cattle of Geryon

Hercules cheated in two labors—the boy Iolaus helped him kill the Hydra, and the rivers, not Hercules, cleaned out Augeas' stables. Two labors were added, making a total of twelve.

The Eleventh Labor—apple tree in the garden of the Hesperides (nymphs)

Hercules sets Prometheus free

Hercules tricks Atlas

The Twelfth Labor—Cerberus and the Underworld

Theseus and the Minotaur

Stories of Theseus and how he faced the Minotaur in the labyrinth can be found in the following:

Fisher, Leonard Everett, author and illus. *Theseus and the Minotaur.* New York: Holiday House, 1988.

Ford, James Evelyn. *Theseus and the Minotaur.* Illus. by Gary Andrews. Minneapolis, MN: Picture Window, 2005.

Hutton, Warwick, illus. *Theseus and the Minotaur.* New York: Margaret K. McElderry, 1989.

VI. Picture Books and Easy Fiction Book Lists

Picture Books for Five- to Six-Year-Olds

Ahlberg, Janet, author and illus., and Allan Ahlberg. *Funnybones.* New York: Greenwillow, 1980.

Asch, Frank. *Turtle Tale.* New York: Dial, 1978.

Balian, Lorna. *Humbug Witch.* New York: Abingdon, 1965.

Barry, Robert E. *Mr. Willowby's Christmas Tree.* New York: McGraw-Hill, 1963.

Brandenberg, Franz. *I Wish I Was Sick, Too!* Illus. by Aliki. New York: Greenwillow, 1976.

Bright, Robert. *Georgie.* Garden City, NY: Doubleday Doran, 1944.

Bright, Robert. *Georgie and the Noisy Ghost.* Garden City, NY: Doubleday, 1971.

Bright, Robert. *Georgie and the Robbers.* Garden City, NY: Doubleday, 1963.

Brown, Margaret Wise. *The Runaway Bunny.* Illus. by Clement Hurd. New York: Harper and Row, 1972.

Burton, Virginia Lee. *The Little House.* Boston: Houghton Mifflin, 1942.

Carle, Eric. *The Very Hungry Caterpillar.* New York: Philomel, 1987.

Charlip, Remy, author and illus., and Burton Supree. *Mother Mother I Feel Sick.* New York: Simon and Schuster, 1966.

Cohen, Miriam. *Will I Have a Friend?* Illus. by Lillian Hoban. New York: Macmillan, 1967.

Cooney, Barbara. *Peter's Long Walk.* Illus. by Lee Kingman. Garden City, NY: Doubleday, 1953.

Craig, M. Jean. *The Dragon in the Clock Box.* Illus. by Kelly Oechsli. New York: Norton, 1962.

Crowe, Robert L. *Clyde Monster.* Illus. by Kay Chorao. New York: Dutton, 1976.

Crowe, Robert L. *Tyler Toad and the Thunder.* Illus. by Kay Chorao. New York: Dutton, 1980.

Crowther, Robert. *The Most Amazing Hide and Seek Alphabet Book.* Middlesex, Eng.: Kestrel, 1977.

Crowther, Robert. *The Most Amazing Hide-and-Seek Counting Book.* Harmondsworth, Middlesex: Kestrel, 1981.

Duke, Kate. *The Guinea Pig ABC.* New York: Dutton, 1983.

Eastman, P. D. *Are You My Mother?* New York: Beginner, 1960.

Eastman, P. D. *The Best Nest.* New York: Beginner, 1968.

Flack, Marjorie. *The Story about Ping.* Illus. by Kurt Wiese. New York: Viking, 1933.

Freeman, Don. *Corduroy.* New York: Viking, 1968.

Gág, Wanda. *Millions of Cats.* New York: Coward-McCann, 1928.

Ginsburg, Mirra. *Good Morning, Chick.* Illus. by Byron Barton. New York: Greenwillow, 1980.

Guilfoile, Elizabeth. *Nobody Listens to Andrew.* Illus. by Mary Stevens. Chicago: Follett, 1957.

Heyward, DuBose. *The Country Bunny and the Little Gold Shoes: As Told to Jenifer.* Illus. by Marjorie Flack. Boston: Houghton Mifflin, 1939.

Hill, Eric. *Spot's First Walk.* New York: Putnam, 1981.

Hoban, Russell. *Bedtime for Frances.* Illus. by Garth Williams. New York: HarperTrophy, 1960.

Hoban, Russell. *The Little Brute Family.* Illus. by Lillian Hoban. New York: Macmillan, 1966.

Hurd, Clement. *The Race.* New York: Random House, 1940.

Hutchins, Pat. *Rosie's Walk.* New York: Macmillan, 1968.

Hutchins, Pat. *Titch.* New York: Macmillan, 1971.

Jensen, Virginia Allen. *Sara and the Door.* Illus. by Ann Strugnell. Reading, MA: Addison-Wesley, 1977.

Joslin, Sesyle. *What Do You Say, Dear?* Illus. by Maurice Sendak. New York: Young Scott, 1958.

Kalan, Robert. *Jump, Frog, Jump!* Illus. by Byron Barton. New York: Greenwillow, 1981.

Keats, Ezra Jack. *Peter's Chair.* New York: Harper and Row, 1967.

Keats, Ezra Jack. *The Snowy Day.* New York: Viking, 1962.

Konkle, Janet. *The Christmas Kitten.* Chicago: Children's Press, 1953.

Levine, Joan Goldman. *A Bedtime Story.* Illus. by Gail Owens. New York: Dutton, 1975.

Lindgren, Barbro. *The Wild Baby.* Illus. by Eva Eriksson. New York: Greenwillow, 1981.

Martin, Bill. *Brown Bear, Brown Bear.* Illus. by Eric Carle. New York: Holt, 1992.

Mayer, Mercer. *Four Frogs in a Box.* New York: Dial, 1967.

Mayer, Mercer. *There's a Nightmare in My Closet.* New York: Dial, 1968.

Mayer, Mercer, and Marianna Mayer, author and illus. *One Frog Too Many.* New York: Dial, 1975.

McCloskey, Robert. *Make Way for Ducklings.* New York: Viking, 1941.

McPhail, David. *The Bear's Toothache.* Boston: Little, Brown, 1972.

Piper, Watty. *The Little Engine That Could.* Illus. by Loren Long. New York: Philomel, 2005.

Potter, Beatrix. *Peter Rabbit.* New York: Frederick Warne, 1996.

Revius, Jacobus. *Noah's Ark.* Illus. by Peter Spier. Garden City, NY: Doubleday, 1977.

Rey, H. A. *Curious George.* Boston: Houghton Mifflin, 1969.

Sendak, Maurice. *Nutshell Library.* New York: Harper and Row, 1962.

Sendak, Maurice. *Nutshell Library. Alligators All Around / Chicken Soup with Rice / One Was Johnny / Pierre.* New York: Harper and Row, 1962.

Sendak, Maurice. *Where the Wild Things Are.* New York: Harper and Row, 1963.

Seuss, Dr. *Horton Hatches the Egg.* New York: Random House, 1940.

Seuss, Dr. *If I Ran the Zoo.* New York: Random House, 1950.

Seuss, Dr. *Thidwick, the Big-Hearted Moose.* New York: Random House, 1975.

Slobodkina, Esphyr. *Caps for Sale: A Tale of a Peddler, Some Monkeys and Their Monkey Business.* New York: W. R. Scott, 1947.

Stone, Jon. *The Monster at the End of This Book: Starring Lovable, Furry Old Grover.* Illus. by Michael Smollin. New York: CTW/Random House, 2000.

Turkle, Brinton. *Thy Friend, Obadiah.* New York: Viking, 1969.

Turkle, Brinton, author and illus., Ann Durrell, ed. *Deep in the Forest.* New York: Dutton, 1976.

Viorst, Judith. *I'll Fix Anthony.* Illus. by Arnold Lobel. New York: Harper and Row, 1969.

Waber, Bernard. *Ira Sleeps Over.* Boston: Houghton Mifflin, 1972.

Wadham, Tim. *The Queen of France.* Illus. by Kady MacDonald Denton. Somerville, MA: Candlewick, 2011.

Wahl, Jan. *Dracula's Cat and Frankenstein's Dog.* Illus. by Kay Chorao. New York: Simon and Schuster Books for Young Readers, 1990.

Ward, Lynd. *The Biggest Bear.* Boston: Houghton Mifflin, 1952.

Wells, Rosemary. *Morris' Disappearing Bag.* New York: Dial, 1975.

Wells, Rosemary. *Timothy Goes to School.* New York: Dial, 1981.

Williams, Barbara. *Albert's Toothache.* Illus. by Kay Chorao. New York: Dutton, 1974.

Wood, Audrey. *The Napping House.* Illus. by Don Wood. San Diego: Harcourt Brace Jovanovich, 1984.

Picture Books for Seven-Year-Olds

Ahlberg, Janet, and Allan Ahlberg. *Each Peach Pear Plum: An "I Spy" Story*. New York: Viking, 1979.

Alexander, Martha G. *Maybe a Monster*. New York: Dial, 1968.

Allard, Harry. *Bumps in the Night*. Illus. by James Marshall. Garden City, NY: Doubleday, 1979.

Allard, Harry. *Miss Nelson Is Back*. Illus. by James Marshall. Boston: Houghton Mifflin, 1982.

Allard, Harry. *Miss Nelson Is Missing!* Illus. by James Marshall. Boston: Houghton Mifflin, 1977.

Allard, Harry. *The Stupids Die*. Illus. by James Marshall. Boston: Houghton Mifflin, 1981.

Anderson, C. W. *Billy and Blaze*. New York: Macmillan, 1962.

Baker, Alan. *Benjamin's Book: Story and Pictures*. New York: Lothrop, Lee and Shepard, 1982.

Balian, Lorna. *The Animal*. Nashville: Abingdon, 1972.

Balian, Lorna. *Bah! Humbug?* Nashville: Abingdon, 1977.

Barrett, Judi. *Animals Should Definitely Not Wear Clothing*. Illus. by Ron Barrett. New York: Atheneum, 1970.

Bates, Lucy. *Little Rabbit's Loose Tooth*. Illus. by Diane De Groat. New York: Crown, 1975.

Bemelmans, Ludwig. *Madeline*. New York: Viking, 1967.

Bishop, Bonnie. *No One Noticed Ralph*. Illus. by Jack Kent. New York: Doubleday, 1979.

Bishop, Claire Huchet. *The Five Chinese Brothers*. Illus. by Kurt Wiese. New York: Coward-McCann, 1938.

Brandenberg, Franz. *I Wish I Was Sick, Too!* Illus. by Aliki. New York: Greenwillow, 1976.

Brown, Marc. *Arthur's Eyes*. Boston: Little, Brown, 1979.

Brown, Marc. *Arthur's Nose*. Boston: Little, Brown, 1976.

Brown, Ruth. *A Dark, Dark Tale: Story and Pictures*. New York: Dial, 1981.

Bryant, Sara Cone. *Epanimondas and His Auntie*. Boston: Houghton Mifflin, 1938.

Burton, Virginia Lee. *Katy and the Big Snow*. Boston: Houghton Mifflin, 1943.

Burton, Virginia Lee. *The Little House*. Boston: Houghton Mifflin, 1942.

Byars, Betsy Cromer. *Go and Hush the Baby*. Illus. by Emily Arnold McCully. New York: Viking, 1971.

Cameron, Polly. *"I Can't" Said the Ant: A Second Book of Nonsense*. New York: Coward-McCann, 1961.

Chorao, Kay. *Molly's Lies*. New York: Seabury, 1979.

Christian Andersen, Hans. *The Ugly Duckling.* Illus. by Jerry Pinkney. New York: Morrow Junior Books, 1999.

Cohen, Miriam. *No Good in Art.* Illus. by Lillian Hoban. New York: Greenwillow, 1980.

Daugherty, James. *Andy and the Lion.* New York: Viking, 1938.

Davis, Alice Vaught. *Timothy Turtle.* Illus. by Guy Brown Wiser. New York: Harcourt, Brace, 1940.

DeLage, Ida. *The Farmer and the Witch.* Champaign, IL: Garrard, 1966.

dePaola, Tomie, author and illus. *Nana Upstairs and Nana Downstairs.* New York: Putnam, 1973.

dePaola, Tomie, author and illus. *Now One Foot, Now the Other.* New York: Putnam, 1981.

de Regniers, Beatrice Schenk. *May I Bring a Friend?* Illus. by Beni Montresor. New York: Atheneum, 1964.

Duke, Kate. *The Guinea Pig ABC.* New York: Dutton, 1983.

Freeman, Don. *Fly High, Fly Low.* New York: Viking, 1957.

Gackenbach, Dick. *Harry and the Terrible Whatzit.* New York: Seabury, 1977.

Gramatsky, Hardie. *Little Toot.* Tadworth, Surrey: World's Work, 1967.

Heide, Florence Parry. *Some Things Are Scary.* Illus. by Jules Feiffer. Cambridge, MA: Candlewick, 2000.

Heine, Helme, author and illus. *Friends.* New York: Atheneum, 1982.

Heine, Helme, author and illus. *The Most Wonderful Egg in the World.* New York: Atheneum, 1983.

Hoban, Russell. *A Birthday for Frances.* Illus. by Lillian Hoban. New York: Harper and Row, 1968.

Hoban, Russell. *Bread and Jam for Frances.* Illus. by Lillian Hoban. New York: Harper and Row, 1964.

Hutchins, Pat, author and illus. *The Very Worst Monster.* New York: Greenwillow, 1985.

Krasilovsky, Phyllis. *The Man Who Didn't Wash His Dishes.* Illus. by Barbara Cooney. Garden City, NY: Doubleday, 1950.

Kraus, Robert. *Leo the Late Bloomer.* Illus. by José Aruego. New York: Windmill, 1971.

Krauss, Ruth. *The Carrot Seed.* Illus. by Crockett Johnson. Toronto: Scholastic, 1945.

Lionni, Leo. *Alexander and the Wind-up Mouse.* New York: Pantheon, 1969.

Lionni, Leo. *Frederick.* New York: Pantheon, 1967.

Lobel, Arnold. *Frog and Toad Are Friends.* New York: Harper and Row, 1970.

Lobel, Arnold. *Frog and Toad Together.* New York: Harper and Row, 1972.

Mahy, Margaret. *The Boy Who Was Followed Home.* Illus. by Steven Kellogg. New York: F. Watts, 1975.

McCloskey, Robert. *Blueberries for Sal.* New York: Viking, 1948.

Minarik, Else Holmelund. *Little Bear.* Illus. by Maurice Sendak. New York: Harper & Brothers, 1957.

Ness, Evaline, author and illus. *Sam, Bangs, and Moonshine.* New York: Holt, Rinehart and Winston, 1966.

Noble, Trinka Hakes. *The Day Jimmy's Boa Ate the Wash.* Illus. by Steven Kellogg. New York: Dial, 1980.

Paterson, Diane. *Smile for Auntie.* New York: Dial, 1976.

Sadler, Marilyn. *Alistair's Elephant.* Illus. by Roger Bollen. Englewood Cliffs, NJ: Prentice-Hall, 1983.

Selden, George. *Sparrow Socks.* Illus. by Peter J. Lippman. New York: Harper and Row, 1965.

Seuss, Dr. *The 500 Hats of Bartholomew Cubbins.* New York: Vanguard, 1938.

Sharmat, Marjorie Weinman. *Little Devil Gets Sick.* Illus. by Marylin Hafner. Garden City, NY: Doubleday, 1980.

Sharmat, Marjorie Weinman. *Scarlet Monster Lives Here.* Illus. by Dennis Kendrick. New York: Harper and Row, 1979.

Steig, William, author and illus. *The Amazing Bone.* New York: Farrar, Straus and Giroux, 1976.

Steig, William, author and illus. *Sylvester and the Magic Pebble.* New York: Windmill, 1969.

Udry, Janice May. *Let's Be Enemies.* Illus. by Maurice Sendak. New York: Harper and Row, 1961.

Viorst, Judith. *Alexander and the Terrible, Horrible, No Good, Very Bad Day.* Illus. by Kay Chorao. Illus. by Ray Cruz. New York: Atheneum, 1972.

Viorst, Judith. *My Mama Says There Aren't Any Zombies, Ghosts, Vampires, Creatures, Demons, Monsters, Fiends, Goblins, or Things.* Illus. by Kay Charao. New York: Atheneum, 1973.

Wells, Rosemary. *Max's First Word.* New York: Dial, 1979.

Wells, Rosemary. *Max's New Suit.* New York: Dial, 1979.

Wells, Rosemary. *Noisy Nora.* New York: Dial Books for Young Readers, 1997.

Wittman, Sally. *Pelly and Peak.* New York: Harper and Row, 1978.

Zion, Gene. *Harry, the Dirty Dog.* Illus. by Margaret Bloy Graham. New York: Harper & Brothers., 1956.

Zolotow, Charlotte. *The Bunny Who Found Easter.* Illus. by Helen Craig. Boston: Houghton Mifflin, 1998.

Meet the Authors

- Introduce the work of Arnold Lobel.
- Introduce the work of Beatrix Potter.
- Introduce the work of Stan Berenstain and Jan Berenstain.

VII. Fiction Book List

Allsburg, Chris Van. *Jumanji.* Boston: Houghton Mifflin, 1981.

Barrett, Judi. *Cloudy with a Chance of Meatballs.* Illus. by Ron Barrett. New York: Atheneum, 1988.

Blegvad, Lenore. *The Great Hamster Hunt.* Illus. by Erik Blegvad. New York: Harcourt, Brace and World, 1969.

Briggs, Raymond. *Jim and the Beanstalk.* New York: Coward-McCann, 1970.

Calhoun, Mary. *Cross-Country Cat.* Illus. by Erick Ingraham. New York: Morrow, 1979.

Calhoun, Mary. *Hot-Air Henry.* Illus. by Erick Ingraham. New York: Morrow, 1981.

Cohen, Barbara. *The Carp in the Bathtub.* Illus. by Joan Halpern. New York: Lothrop, Lee and Shepard, 1972.

Conford, Ellen. *Impossible, Possum.* Illus. by Rosemary Wells. Boston: Little, Brown, 1971.

Cooney, Barbara. *Miss Rumphius.* New York: Viking, 1982.

DeLage, Ida. *The Old Witch Goes to the Ball.* Illus. by Gustave E. Nebel. Champaign, IL: Garrard, 1969.

Delton, Judy. *Two Good Friends.* Illus. by Giulio Maestro. New York: Crown, 1974.

dePaola, Tomie, author and illus. *Bill and Pete Go down the Nile.* New York: Putnam, 1987.

Elting, Mary, and Michael Folsom. *Q Is for Duck: An Alphabet Guessing Game.* Illus. by Jack Kent. New York: Houghton Mifflin/Clarion, 1980.

Flora, James. *Wanda and the Bumbly Wizard.* New York: Atheneum, 1980.

Gage, Wilson. *Squash Pie.* Illus. by Glen Rounds. New York: Greenwillow, 1976.

Gantos, Jack *Rotten Ralph.* Illus. by Nicole Rubel. Boston: Houghton Mifflin, 1976.

Giff, Patricia Reilly. *Today Was a Terrible Day.* Illus. by Susanna Natti. New York: Viking, 1980.

Greenberg, David. *Slugs.* Illus. by Victoria Chess. Boston: Little, Brown, 1983.

Heide, Florence Parry. *The Shrinking of Treehorn.* Illus. by Edward Gorey. New York: Holiday House, 1971.

Heide, Florence Parry. *Treehorn's Treasure.* Illus. by Edward Gorey. New York: Holiday House, 1981.

Hoguet, Susan Ramsay. *I Unpacked My Grandmother's Trunk: A Picture Book Game.* New York: Dutton, 1983.

Hutton, Warwick. *Jonah and the Great Fish.* New York: Atheneum, 1983.

Keats, Ezra Jack. *Goggles!* New York: Macmillan, 1969.

Leaf, Munro. *The Story of Ferdinand.* Illus. by Robert Lawson. New York: Viking, 1936.

Lionni, Leo. *Tico and the Golden Wings.* New York: Pantheon, 1964.

Low, Joseph, author and illus. *Mice Twice.* New York: Atheneum, 1980.

Marshall, James. *George and Martha.* Boston: Houghton Mifflin, 1972.

Mayne, William. *The Patchwork Cat.* Illus. by Nicola Bayley. New York: Knopf, 1981.

Merrill, Jean. *The Elephant Who Liked to Smash Small Cars.* Illus. by Ronni Solbert. New York: Pantheon, 1967.

Minarik, Else Holmelund. *No Fighting, No Biting!* Illus. by Maurice Sendak. New York: Harper & Brothers, 1958.

Ness, Evaline. *Sam, Bangs, and Moonshine.* New York: Holt, Rinehart and Winston, 1966.

Oppenheim, Joanne. *Mrs. Peloki's Class Play.* Illus. by Joyce Audy Zarins. New York: Dodd, Mead, 1984.

Parish, Peggy. *Amelia Bedelia.* Illus. by Fritz Siebel. New York: Harper and Row, 1963.

Parish, Peggy. *Zed and the Monsters.* Illus. by Paul Galdone. Garden City, NY: Doubleday, 1979.

Peet, Bill. *Buford, the Little Big Horn.* Boston: Houghton Mifflin, 1967.

Peet, Bill. *Hubert's Hair-raising Adventure.* Boston: Houghton Mifflin, 1959.

Peet, Bill. *The Whingdingdilly.* Boston: Houghton Mifflin, 1970.

Peet, Bill. *The Wump World.* Boston: Houghton-Mifflin, 1970.

Seuss, Dr. *The Lorax.* New York: Random House, 1971.

Shannon, George. *The Gang and Mrs. Higgins.* Illus. by Andrew Vines. New York: Greenwillow, 1981.

Steig, William. *Doctor DeSoto.* Farrar, Straus and Giroux, 1982.

Stevenson, James. *Could Be Worse!* New York: Greenwillow, 1977.

Stevenson, James. *What's under My Bed?* New York: Greenwillow, 1983.

Thurber, James. *Many Moons.* Illus. by Louis Slobodkin. New York: Harcourt Brace and Company, 1943.

Titus, Eve. Anatole. *Illus. by Paul Galdone.* New York: Whittlesey House, 1956.

Warner, Gertrude Chandler. *The Boxcar Children.* Chicago: Albert Whitman, 1977.

Wells, Rosemary. *Benjamin and Tulip.* New York: Dial, 1973.

Williams, Barbara. *Jeremy Isn't Hungry.* Illus. by Martha G. Alexander. New York: Dutton, 1978.

Yolen, Jane. *Commander Toad and the Big Black Hole.* Illus. by Bruce Degen. New York: Coward-McCann, 1983.

Yolen, Jane. *Sleeping Ugly.* Illus. by Diane Stanley. New York: Coward, McCann and Geoghegan, 1981.

Meet the Authors

- Introduce the work of Dr. Seuss.
- Introduce the Caldecott Medal, and share winners of medals and Honor Books.

VIII. Sample Program: Discover the Oz Books

PROGRAM TITLE

Discover the Oz Books by L. Frank Baum

TOPIC

Read-aloud with focused activities based on ideas suggested by the stories.

TARGET AUDIENCE

Ages five–seven

IDEAL AUDIENCE SIZE

Fifteen–twenty

LENGTH OF PROGRAM

Sixty minutes—number of weekly sessions can vary

SETUP TIME

Varies by week, but typically fifteen minutes

PREPROGRAM TIME

Have supplemental materials in place twenty minutes prior to start time for children who arrive early and need something to peruse.

GOALS AND OBJECTIVES FOR THIS SPECIFIC PROGRAM

- Introduce the Oz books to children.
- Help children transition from storytime with parents to more independent listening and learning.

- Develop children's listening skills.
- Increase children's attention level.

L. Frank Baum wrote fourteen Oz books. Here is a list of the books in order:

The Wonderful Wizard of Oz	*Tik-Tok of Oz*
The Marvelous Land of Oz	*The Scarecrow of Oz*
Ozma of Oz	*Rinkitink in Oz*
Dorothy and the Wizard in Oz	*The Lost Princess of Oz*
The Road to Oz	*The Tin Woodman of Oz*
The Emerald City of Oz	*The Magic of Oz*
The Patchwork Girl of Oz	*Glinda of Oz*

Description

Each session begins with reading out loud a section from one of the Oz books. Here is a suggested list of stories from the books that work well as independent read-alouds. The page numbers referenced are from the original editions, reprinted by Books of Wonder:

"A Highly Magnified History (The Wogglebug's Story)"—*The Land of Oz,* p. 147
"Tiktok the Machine Man"—*Ozma of Oz,* p. 37
"The Musiker"—*The Road to Oz,* p. 92
"Race between Jim the Cabhorse and the Sawhorse"—*Dorothy and the Wizard in Oz,* p. 173
"The Loons of Loonvile"—*The Tin Woodman of Oz,* p. 46

From *The Emerald City of Oz:*
"How the Cuttenclips Lived," p. 100
"How They Matched the Fuddles," p. 127 (doing puzzles would be an excellent activity to accompany this chapter, as it involves Dorothy and her companions putting together the Fuddles, who are made out of puzzle pieces that have been scattered; includes puzzle)
"How Dorothy Visited Utensia," p. 169
"How They Came to Bunbury," p. 180
"How They Encountered the Flutterbudgets," p. 237

The read-aloud is followed by a focused activity suggested by the book. At the end of each session, participants contribute to a blog about their experiences with the book and the program. Activities can include the following:

- After reading "How the Cuttenclips Lived," from *The Emerald City of Oz,* do a paper cutout activity.
- After reading "How They Matched the Fuddles," from *The Emerald City of Oz,* have the kids put together some particularly difficult puzzles.

Materials and Preparation

OZ BOOKS FOR READING ALOUD

- Baum, L. Frank. *Dorothy and the Wizard in Oz.* Illus. by John R. Neill. New York: Books of Wonder, 1990.
- Baum, L. Frank. *The Emerald City of Oz.* Illus. by John R. Neill. New York: Morrow, 1993.
- Baum, L. Frank. *The Marvelous Land of Oz: Being an Account of the Further Adventures of the Scarecrow and Tin Woodman.* Illus. by John R. Neill. New York: Morrow, 1985.
- Baum, L. Frank. *Ozma of Oz.* Illus. by John R. Neill. New York: Harper-Collins, 1989.
- Baum, L. Frank. *The Road to Oz.* Illus. by John R. Neill. New York: Books of Wonder, 1991.
- Baum, L. Frank. *The Tin Woodman of Oz.* Illus. by John R. Neill. New York: Morrow, 1999.

SUPPLIES NEEDED

Paper, pencils, scissors, puzzles

EXTRA STAFF NEEDED

Perhaps one other staff member during craft portions of the program

EQUIPMENT NEEDED

None

ROOM SETUP

At one side or half of the story room, provide pillows and bean bags for children to sit on for the read-aloud and discussion portion of the program. For the activity portion, set up tables in the story room.

CORRESPONDING EXHIBIT OR DISPLAY

Display the books listed above, along with any other Oz books by Baum, as well as any other Oz-related books you might have in your collection that would be appropriate for a younger registrant.

CONTINGENCY PLANS

- Too few registrants (four or fewer): Contact those registered and encourage them to get a friend to register with them.
- Too many registrants (more than twenty): Take names, and if at least six are on the list, offer to split into two groups and run the program twice.
- Primary librarian unavailable to lead: Another librarian will be able to use these program plans as a substitute.

- Computers are down: Skip blog entry for the day. Share and discuss other print resources if planned online activities are not accessible.

PROGRAM PLANNING CALENDAR

Use the blank calendar format in figure 2.1 to plan a multiweek program.

Poetry to Share with Oz

Use any of the poetry in the poetry section of this chapter.

Figure 2.1 **Program Planning Calendar**

Week	Read-Aloud Chapter	Poetry	Activity	Supplies Needed	Notes
1					
2					
3					
4					
5					

Chapter 3

Wordplay for
Eight- to Twelve-Year-Olds

—•—————•—

Programming for eight- to twelve-year-olds is at the heart of the idea behind school librarian Katie Blake's Childread program and now *Wordplay for Kids*. With the emphasis on the Every Child Ready to Read @ your library tool kit, and at the opposite end, on teen centers and programming, this middle group has truly become lost. Young adult literature may be booming with its paranormal romance and dystopian dramas, but there is less and less true early- to middle-grade fiction being written and published. Even the Newbery winners over the past decade or so have seemed for the most part to skew older. There have certainly been rare, welcome exceptions, such as *When You Reach Me*, but for the most part, these kids have been left out in the proverbial cold.

That is one of the reasons why, for this section, you will find that many of the books referenced are older and in many cases out of print. I make no excuses for skewing older. The books referenced in this section should not be relegated to the dust heap of time but deserve to be read and loved by generation after generation. There is too much of the tremendous heritage of children's literature that is being lost to memory and forgotten over time. Many of these books may still be in libraries or can be obtained online through Amazon, Half.com, Powell's Books, or other retailers of secondhand books.

The ideal Wordplay for Kids program for this age group will be a multi-week ongoing session with children coming to the library at least once a week for a program. The program should begin with choral poetry reading, followed by reading out loud. Finally, there is an activity based on something suggested by the book. This section provides various resources to put together a Wordplay for Kids series.

I. Poetry

Since each Wordplay for Kids program should begin with choral poetry reading, the poetry comes first. I have found that when you delve into poetry, as stated previously, you should never underestimate a child's ability to understand. Thus, you will find a number of longer classic narrative poems, such "The Charge of the Light Brigade" and "The Highwayman," which defy classification as to a specific age level. Where poems are in the public domain or the text is unavailable anywhere, I have included the full text of the poem. With other poems, still in copyright, I have included the title, author, first line (or lines), and multiple sources where the complete poem may be found. Again, many of the books referenced may be out of print. With poetry, however, there are numerous websites where the complete texts of these poems and many more may be found online. I encourage you to do Google or other web searches for these poems, and you are likely to discover many more along the way. Look for the poems online first before going the secondhand-bookseller route.

The poetry selections are divided into different topics, such as "Nature and Seasons" and "People and Things." There are also poems for holidays as well. Katie Blake would take one of these poems, get the children to master it, and then go on to another. However, she would always go back and have the children read together out loud all the poems they had previously learned. If you are doing a multi-week program, you can try to build on the poetry each week.

II. Fiction

This is a book list of older books that ought to be shared with today's children. It is divided into three sets of books with increasing difficulty, which can be introduced one at a time.

III. Folk and Fairy Stories

Eight- to twelve-year-olds are not too old to hear folktales and fairy tales. They need this cultural literacy as much as the five- to seven-year-old set. This book list includes more complex and sometimes darker tales appropriate for this age group.

IV. Programs

This section includes suggested programs in different formats. The blank program template, provided in chapter 3's "After School Programs," can help with planning. Wordplay for Kids programs can work a few different ways.

I begin with examples of multi-week programs based on a particular theme, such as fantasies or mysteries. In this case, choose short stories or short sections of longer books to read out loud.

One of my favorite options is to devote an entire program reading one book out loud. To do this, you need to look at the length of the book and calculate how many pages or chapters you will have to read each session to complete the book. The *Hugo Cabret* program is an example of a successful program based on a single book that I presented in an Arizona library. The program captivated a group of children to the extent that they wanted to read the book out loud themselves at each session. The *Chasing Vermeer* program is another example.

Another option is to focus on the work of a specific author and highlight a chapter from an individual book each week. At my library in Washington State, we have held successful programs highlighting the books of a local author, Suzanne Selfors as well as Wendelin Van Draanen. The Suzanne Selfors program concluded with a visit by the author. Although authors may not be available to come in person, you may be able to arrange Skype visits or other ways for the children participating in the program to interact directly with the author.

I. Poetry

Fundamentals of Poetry

Introducing Poetry

Tell students that poetry is like a can of frozen orange juice. Add three cans of water and you get prose.

Poetry has also been described variously as "the kind of language that says more and says it more intensely than other language" or "words arranged in a rhythmic pattern with regular accents" or "words carefully selected for sound, accent and meaning . . . to express imaginatively ideas and emotions."

Explain that the purpose of poetry is to increase awareness of life, to give pleasure.

When introducing the choral reading of poetry, you may wish to highlight any of the following elements found in all poetry:

1. Rhythm
2. Melody, rhyme, alliteration
3. Imagery
4. Form
5. Sound (of language)

Three books of poetry have won the Newbery Medal: *A Visit to William Blake's Inn: Poems for Innocent and Experienced Travelers*, by Nancy Willard (1981); *Joyful Noise: Poems for Two Voices*, by Paul Fleischman (1988); and *Good Masters! Sweet Ladies! Voices from a Medieval Village*, by Laura Amy Schlitz (2007). The poems in Fleischman's *Joyful Noise: Poems for Two Voices* are difficult but a challenge and a delight for kids to perform out loud.

My experience sharing poetry with children has shown that the wordplay that is at the heart of poetry is tremendously appealing to children. Perhaps my favorite book of poetry is Arnold Lobel's *Whiskers & Rhymes* (New York: Greenwillow, 1985).

It contains inspired verse like "Books to the ceiling / books to the sky," which is a poem that I've shared regularly at the beginning of my preschool storytimes. This book is truly one for the ages, a masterpiece of language that should be at the heart of any poetry collection.

Children love poetry naturally, because they respond to the sounds of the words, and it helps them develop a love of language. That is why they love nursery rhymes and children's songs. However, when children get to school, poetry is often presented as something that has to be memorized or analyzed for its meaning, and it can create a bad taste in children's mouths. I recall a class where we ripped apart the poetry of e. e. cummings. Poems that at first enchanted me became so many words on a page and lost their wonder.

Presenting poetry as fun in a choral-reading context can help avoid children gaining a permanent bias against poetry. Poetry is truly meant to be heard rather than read silently. Through choral poetry reading, children can play around with words and sounds. Choral poetry reading allows children to both hear and manipulate language. Some types of poems that might otherwise be deadly dull can spring to life when performed as a choral reading. Poems can be divided into speaking parts for individual children or for groups. As you introduce the poems in this book to children, make sure that it is fun and not associated with work.

Narrative poems and limericks should be presented, as these are some of the most popular forms of poetry with children. Of course, children will favor poems that contain the elements mentioned previously: rhyme, rhythm, and sound. Humorous poetry will also work well, as will poems that put a new spin on familiar experiences. Animal poems can also be favorites.

Shel Silverstein's *Where the Sidewalk Ends*, along with his other collections, is still one of the most popular books of poetry for children. Silverstein's poems are edgy and have a sense of opposition to authority and a feeling of being a bit dangerous that children pick on immediately. Another popular children's poet whose body of work is quite significant is Jack Prelutsky.

Forms of Poetry

Explain that the difference between poetry and prose is in most cases because poetry has a specific pattern or set form, like a sonnet or a haiku. The poems in this book encompass many of the familiar poetic forms:

Narrative Poems
These poems tell a story in poetic form. The "Classics" section includes examples of this form, such as "Paul Revere's Ride."

Limericks
Children will certainly be familiar with the scansion of a limerick, with its familiar rhyme scheme. Limericks are usually funny poems, and they notably appeared early on, in Edward Lear's *Book of Nonsense*, published in 1846. Here's an example:

> A thrifty young fellow of Shoreham
> Made brown paper trousers and woreham;
> He looked nice and neat
> Till he bent in the street
> To pick up a pin; then he toreham.

Concrete Poems
Some of the poems included in this collection are known as "concrete" poems, which are poems printed on the page with the words creating a shape that also represents the subject of the poem. An example from this collection is "The Neck of a Running Giraffe," by Shel Silverstein, which approximates the shape of a giraffe's neck, on which the narrator of the poem is attempting, with limited success, to write. A concrete poem is written or printed on the page. This is the one form of poetry that is not just about the sound of the language but one that has to be seen to be appreciated.

Other Forms of Poetry
Other forms of poetry that can be presented to children include haiku, lyric poetry, and free verse. Haiku is perhaps the most well known, and the most overused. Haiku has a deceptively simple syllabic structure but is actually devilishly complex. Lyric poetry can be defined as poetry that feels more like song lyrics, and, in fact, one of its defining features is that it can be set to or

accompanied by music. Lyric poems are also distinguished by their emotional and personal subject matter. Free verse, of course, is poetry that doesn't rhyme and really follows no rules. And there are many more. There is William Shakespeare's signature iambic pentameter and the sonnet form, of which he was a master. The key is for children to understand the basics of the form but not to lose the magic of the words.

Building a Poetry Collection

In this collection, anthologies are often cited as a source for the poems. Perhaps the premier anthology for young people is *The Random House Book of Poetry*, with poems selected by Jack Prelutsky and lovingly illustrated by Arnold Lobel. This is arguably Lobel's masterwork and one of his most important legacies. And that is saying a lot, considering he was the author of the *Frog and Toad* books as well as books of his original poetry, including *Pigericks* (pig limericks) and *Whiskers and Rhymes*. Other anthologies upon which I heavily rely include *Sing a Song of Popcorn,* edited by Marcia Brown and Beatrice Schenk de Regniers, with illustrations by nine different artists, all connected by the fact that they have won the Caldecott Medal. Another collection, edited by Jack Prelutsky, who is probably the king of American children's poetry, is *Read-Aloud Rhymes for the Very Young,* which is illustrated by the Arthur the Aardvark creator, Marc Brown.

Also referenced are many collections of poems by a single author, such as Karla Kuskin and Judith Viorst. There are also many examples of single poems illustrated in picture-book format. One terrific example is "Stopping by Woods on a Snowy Evening," by Robert Frost, illustrated by Susan Jeffers.

The following core poetry collection provides plenty of material for Wordplay for Kids programming.

Adoff, Arnold. *Black Is Brown Is Tan.* Illus. by Emily Arnold McCully. New York: Harper and Row, 1973.

Baylor, Byrd. *I'm in Charge of Celebrations.* Illus. by Peter Parnall. New York: Scribner's, 1986.

Cassedy, Sylvia. *Roomrimes: Poems.* Illus. by Michele Chessare. New York: Crowell, 1987.

Chandra, Deborah. *Balloons and Other Poems.* Illus. by Leslie W. Bowman. New York: Farrar, Straus and Giroux, 1990.

Ciardi, John. *You Read to Me, I'll Read to You.* Illus. by Edward Gorey. Philadelphia: Lippincott, 1962.

de Regniers, Beatrice Schenk, ed. *Sing a Song of Popcorn: Every Child's Book of Poems.* Illus. by Marcia Brown. New York: Scholastic, 1988.

Esbensen, Barbara Juster. *Who Shrank My Grandmother's House? Poems of Discovery*. Illus. by Eric Beddows. New York: HarperCollins, 1992.

Fleischman, Paul. *Joyful Noise: Poems for Two Voices*. Illus. by Eric Beddows. New York: Harper and Row, 1988.

Frost, Robert. *Stopping by Woods on a Snowy Evening*. Illus. by Susan Jeffers. New York: Dutton, 1978.

Greenfield, Eloise. *Honey, I Love, and Other Poems*. Illus. by Diane Dillon, and Leo Dillon. New York: HarperCollins, 2003.

Hopkins, Lee Bennett. *More Surprises*. Illus. by Megan Lloyd. New York: Harper and Row, 1987.

Kennedy, X. J. *Brats*. Illus. by James Watts. New York: Atheneum, 1986.

Kuskin, Karla. *Dogs & Dragons, Trees & Dreams: A Collection of Poems*. New York: Harper and Row, 1980.

Larrick, Nancy. *Piping down the Valleys Wild: Poetry for the Young of All Ages*. Illus. by Ellen Raskin. New York: Bantam Doubleday Dell Books for Young Readers, 1999.

Lewis, J. Patrick. *A Hippopotamusn't and Other Animal Verses*. Illus. by Victoria Chess. New York: Dial Books for Young Readers, 1990.

Livingston, Myra Cohn. *Celebrations*. Illus. by Leonard Everett Fisher. New York: Holiday House, 1985.

Longfellow, Henry Wadsworth. *Paul Revere's Ride*. Illus. by Ted Rand and Barbara Powderly. New York: Dutton Children's Books, 1990.

McCord, David Thompson Watson. *One at a Time*. Illus. by Henry B. Kane. Boston: Little, Brown, 1977.

Merriam, Eve. *Fresh Paint: New Poems*. Illus. by David Frampton. New York: Macmillan, 1986.

Merriam, Eve. *Halloween A B C*. Illus. by Lane Smith. New York: Macmillan, 1987.

Moore, Lilian. *Something New Begins: New and Selected Poems*. New York: Atheneum, 1982.

Nash, Ogden. *Custard and Company: Poems*. Illus. by Quentin Blake. Boston: Little, Brown, 1980.

Prelutsky, Jack. *The New Kid on the Block: Poems*. Illus. by James Stevenson. New York: Greenwillow, 1984.

Prelutsky, Jack. *Nightmares: Poems to Trouble Your Sleep*. Illus. by Arnold Lobel. New York: Greenwillow, 1976.

Prelutsky, Jack, ed. *The Random House Book of Poetry for Children*. Illus. by Arnold Lobel. New York: Random House, 1983.

Prelutsky, Jack, ed. *Read-Aloud Rhymes for the Very Young*. Illus. by Marc Brown. New York: Knopf, 1986.

Service, Robert W. *The Cremation of Sam McGee*. Illus. by Ted Harrison. New York: Greenwillow, 1987.

Siebert, Diane. *Heartland.* Illus. by Wendell Minor. New York: Crowell, 1989.

Silverstein, Shel, author and illus. *Where the Sidewalk Ends: The Poems & Drawings of Shel Silverstein.* New York: Harper and Row, 1974.

Volavková, Hana. *I Never Saw Another Butterfly: Children's Drawings and Poems from Terezín Concentration Camp, 1942–1944.* New York: Schocken, 1993.

Worth, Valerie. *All the Small Poems.* Illus. by Natalie Babbitt. New York: Farrar, Strauss and Giroux, 1987.

Yolen, Jane. *Bird Watch: A Book of Poetry.* Illus. by Ted Lewin. New York: Philomel, 1990.

Poetry for Choral Reading

Topic: Animals

"The Little Turtle"   *by Vachel Lindsay*

There was a little turtle.
He lived in a box.
He swam in a puddle.
He climbed on the rocks.

He snapped at a mosquito.
He snapped at a flea.
He snapped at a minnow.
And he snapped at me.

He caught the mosquito.
He caught the flea.
He caught the minnow.
But he didn't catch me.

"If You Ever, Ever, Ever Meet a Grizzly Bear"   *by Mary Austin*

If you ever, ever, ever meet a grizzly bear,
You must never, never, never ask him where
He is going,
Or *what* he is doing;
For if you ever, ever dare
To stop a grizzly bear,
You will never meet *another* grizzly bear.

This poem can be found in the following:
> Ferris, Helen Josephine. *Favorite Poems: Old and New.* Illus. by Leonard
> Weisgard. Garden City, NY: Doubleday, 1957.

"Three Gray Geese"   —*Anon.*

> Three gray geese in a green field grazing,
> Gray were the geese and the green was the grazing.

"If You, Like Me"   *by Karla Kuskin*

First lines: "If you, like me, / Were made of fur"

This poem can be found in the following:
> Kuskin, Karla. *Moon, Have You Met My Mother? The Collected Poems of
> Karla Kuskin.* Illus. by Sergio Ruzzier. New York: Laura Geringer, 2003.

"I've Got a Dog as Thin as a Rail"   —*Anon.*

> I've got a dog as thin as a rail,
> He's got fleas all over his tail;
> Every time his tail goes flop,
> The fleas on the bottom all hop to the top.

"Puppy"   *by Robert L. Tyler*

First line: "Catch and shake the cobra garden hose. Scramble on panicky paws
and flee"

This poem can be found in the following:
> Hopkins, Lee Bennett. *A Dog's Life: Poems.* Illus. by Linda Rochester Rich-
> ards. San Diego: Harcourt Brace Jovanovich, 1983.

"Mother Doesn't Want a Dog"   —*Judith Viorst*

First lines: "Mother doesn't want a dog / Mother says they smell"

This poem can be found in the following:
> Baker, Russell, ed. *The Norton Book of Light Verse.* New York: Norton, 1986.
> Prelutsky, Jack, ed. *The Random House Book of Poetry for Children.* Illus. by
> Arnold Lobel. New York: Random House, 1983.

"Meditatio"   *by Ezra Pound*

When I carefully consider the curious habits of dogs
I am compelled to conclude
That man is the superior animal.
When I consider the curious habits of man
I confess, my friend, I am puzzled.

This poem can be found in the following:
www.poemhunter.com/poem/meditatio.

"I Wouldn't"   *by John Ciardi*

First lines: "There's a mouse house / In the hall wall"

This poem can be found in the following:
Janeczko, Paul B. *This Delicious Day: 65 Poems.* New York: Orchard, 1987.
Kennedy, X. J., and Dorothy M. Kennedy. *Talking like the Rain: A Read-to
    Me Book of Poems.* Illus. by Jane Dyer. Boston: Little, Brown, 1992.

"Mice"   *by Rose Fyleman*

First lines: "I think mice / Are rather nice"

This poem can be found in the following:
Fyleman, Rose. *Mice.* Illus. by Lois Ehlert. New York: Beach Lane, 2012.

"About the Teeth of Sharks"   *by John Ciardi*

First lines: "The thing about a shark is—teeth, / One row above, one row beneath"

This poem can be found in the following:
Cole, William. *A Zooful of Animals.* Illus. by Lynn Munsinger. Boston:
    Houghton Mifflin, 1992.
Hall, Donald, ed. *The Oxford Book of Children's Verse in America.* New York:
    Oxford University Press, 1985.
Hall, Donald, ed. *The Oxford Illustrated Book of American Children's Poems.*
    New York: Oxford University Press, 1999.

"The Neck of a Running Giraffe"   *by Shel Silverstein*

First line: "Please do not make fun of me"

This poem can be found in the following:
>Silverstein, Shel, author and illus. *Where the Sidewalk Ends: The Poems & Drawings of Shel Silverstein.* New York: Harper and Row, 1974.

"The Snake" *by Jack Prelutsky*

First lines: "Don't ever make the bad mistake / of stepping on a sleeping snake"

This poem can be found in the following:
>Prelutsky, Jack. *Something Big Has Been Here.* Illus. by James Stevenson. New York: Greenwillow, 1990.

"Boa Constrictor" *by Shel Silverstein*

First line: "Oh, I'm being eaten. By a boa constrictor"

This poem can be found in the following:
>Silverstein, Shel, author and illus. *Where the Sidewalk Ends: The Poems & Drawings of Shel Silverstein.* New York: Harper and Row, 1974.

"Bugs" *by Karla Kuskin*

First line: "I am very fond of bugs"

This poem can be found in the following:
>Kuskin, Karla. *Moon, Have You Met My Mother? The Collected Poems of Karla Kuskin.* Illus. by Sergio Ruzzier. New York: Laura Geringer, 2003.

"The Tickle Rhyme" *by Ian Serallier*

First line: "'Who's that tickling my back?' said the wall"

This poem can be found in the following:
>Cole, William. *An Arkful of Animals.* Illus. by Lynn Munsinger. Boston: Houghton Mifflin, 1978.
>Prelutsky, Jack, ed. *The Random House Book of Poetry for Children.* Illus. by Arnold Lobel. New York: Random House, 1983.

"The Flea" *by Roland Young*

First line: "And here's the happy, bounding flea—"

This poem can be found in the following:
>Young, Roland. *Not for Children, Pictures and Verse.* Garden City, NY: Doubleday, Doran, 1930.

"A Fly and a Flea in a Flue"   *—Anon*

> A fly and a flea in a flue
> Were imprisoned, so what could they do?
> Said the fly, "Let us flee"
> "Let us fly!" said the flea
> And they flew through a flaw in the flue.

"A Bug Sat in a Silver Flower"   *by Karla Kuskin*

First line: "A bug sat in a silver flower"

This poem can be found in the following:
> Kuskin, Karla. *Moon, Have You Met My Mother? The Collected Poems of Karla Kuskin.* Illus. by Sergio Ruzzier. New York: Laura Geringer, 2003.
> Prelutsky, Jack, ed. *The Random House Book of Poetry for Children.* Illus. by Arnold Lobel. New York: Random House, 1983.

"Easy Diver"   *by Robert Froman*

First lines: "Pigeon on the roof. / Dives"

This poem can be found in the following:
> Janeczko, Paul B. *A Poke in the I: A Collection of Concrete Poems.* Illus. by Christopher Raschka. Cambridge, MA: Candlewick, 2001.

"The Animal Fair"   *—Anon*

> I went to the animal fair,
> The birds and the bees were there.
> The big baboon by the light of the moon,
> Was combing his auburn hair.
>
> The monkey, he got drunk,
> And sat on the Elephant's trunk.
> The Elephant sneezed and fell on his knees,
> And what became of the monk, the monk?

"The Animal Store"   *by Rachel Field*

> If I had a hundred dollars to spend,
> Or maybe a little more,
> I'd hurry as fast as my legs would go
> Straight to the animal store.

I wouldn't say, "How much for this or that?"
"What kind of a dog is he?"
I'd buy as many as rolled an eye,
Or wagged a tail at me!

I'd take the hound with the drooping ears
That sits by himself alone;
Cockers and Cairns and wobbly pups
For to be my very own.

I might buy a parrot all red and green,
And the monkey I saw before,
If I had a hundred dollars to spend,
Or maybe a little more.

This poem can be found in the following:
Poetry Foundation, at www.poetryfoundation.org/poem/176942.

"Jump or Jiggle" *by Evelyn Beyer*

First lines: "Frogs jump / Caterpillars hump"

This poem can be found in the following:
Austin, Mary C., and Queenie Beatrice Mills. *The Sound of Poetry.* Boston: Allyn and Bacon, 1963.
Prelutsky, Jack, ed. *Read-Aloud Rhymes for the Very Young.* Illus. by Marc Brown. New York: Knopf, 1986.

"I Never Saw a Purple Cow" *by Gelett Burgess*

I never saw a PURPLE COW,
I never HOPE to see one;
But I can tell you, anyhow,
I'd rather SEE than BE one!

"Algy Met a Bear" *—Anon.*

Algy met a bear,
A bear met Algy.
The bear was bulgy,
The bulge was Algy.

"The Cow" *by Ogden Nash*

First lines: "The cow is of the bovine ilk. / One end is moo, the other milk"

This poem can be found in the following:
Baker, Russell, ed. *The Norton Book of Light Verse.* New York: Norton, 1986.
Prelutsky, Jack, ed. *The Random House Book of Poetry for Children.* Illus. by Arnold Lobel. New York: Random House, 1983.

"The Hedgehog Sleeps beneath the Hedge" *by J. J. Bell*

First lines: "The hedgehog sleeps beneath the hedge / As you may sometimes see—"

This poem can be found in the following:
Prelutsky, Jack, ed. *The Random House Book of Poetry for Children.* Illus. by Arnold Lobel. New York: Random House, 1983.

"Sally and Manda Are Two Little Lizards" *by Alice B. Campbell*

First lines: "Sally and Manda are two little lizards / Who gobble up flies in their two little gizzards"

This poem can be found in the following:
Prelutsky, Jack, ed. *The Random House Book of Poetry for Children.* Illus. by Arnold Lobel. New York: Random House, 1983.

"The Lizard Is a Timid Thing" *by John Gardner*

First lines: "The lizard is a timid thing / That cannot dance or fly or sing"

This poem can be found in the following:
Prelutsky, Jack, ed. *The Random House Book of Poetry for Children.* Illus. by Arnold Lobel. New York: Random House, 1983.

"The Lizard" *by Theodore Roethke*

First lines: "The Time to Tickle a Lizard, / Is Before, or Right After, a Blizzard"

This poem can be found in the following:
Philip, Neil, ed. *The New Oxford Book of Children's Verse.* Oxford: Oxford University Press, 1996.

Prelutsky, Jack, ed. *The Random House Book of Poetry for Children.* Illus. by Arnold Lobel. New York: Random House, 1983.

Roethke, Theodore. *The Collected Poems of Theodore Roethke.* Garden City, NY: Anchor, 1975.

Smith, William Jay. *A Green Place: Modern Poems.* Illus. by Jacques Hnizdovsky. New York: Delacorte/Seymour Lawrence, 1982.

"The Pig" *by Roland Young*

First line: "The pig is not a nervous beast"

This poem can be found in the following:
Prelutsky, Jack, ed. *The Random House Book of Poetry for Children.* Illus. by Arnold Lobel. New York: Random House, 1983.

"There Was a Rude Pig from Duluth" *by Arnold Lobel*

First line: "There was a rude pig from Duluth"

This poem can be found in the following:
Lobel, Arnold. *The Book of Pigericks: Pig Limericks.* New York: Harper and Row, 1983.

"The Gnat" *by Eugene Rudzwiez*

First line: "Gnats are gnumerous"

This poem can be found in the following:
Janeczko, Paul B. *This Delicious Day: 65 Poems.* New York: Orchard, 1987.

"The Vulture" *by Hilaire Belloc*

The Vulture eats between his meals
and that's the reason why
He very, very rarely feels
as well as you and I.

His eye is dull, his head is bald,
his neck is growing thinner.
Oh! what a lesson for us all
who only eat at dinner!

"The Crocodile" *by Lewis Carroll*

> How doth the little crocodile
> Improve his shining tail,
> And pour the waters of the Nile
> On every golden scale!
>
> How cheerfully he seems to grin,
> How neatly spreads his claws,
> And welcomes little fishes in
> With gently smiling jaws!

"The Eagle" *—Alfred Tennyson*

> He clasps the crag with crooked hands;
> Close to the sun in lonely lands,
> Ringed with the azure world, he stands.
> The wrinkled sea beneath him crawls;
> He watches from his mountain walls,
> And like a thunderbolt he falls.

"Soliloquy of a Tortoise Dozing under a Rosetree Near a Beehive at Noon While a Dog Scampers about and a Cuckoo Calls from a Distant Wood" *—E. V. Rieu*

First line: "So far as I can see"

This poem can be found in the following:
> Cole, William, ed. *The Fireside Book of Humorous Poetry*. New York: Simon and Schuster, 1959.

"Night Thought of a Tortoise" *—E. V. Rieu*

First line: "The world is very flat"

This poem can be found in the following:
> Cole, William, ed. *The Fireside Book of Humorous Poetry*. New York: Simon and Schuster, 1959.

"Cats" *(also known as "The Stray Cat")* *—Eve Merriam*

First line: "It's just an old alley cat"

This poem can be found in the following:
Whittier, Sara L. *101 Favorite Cat Poems.* Chicago: Contemporary, 1991.

"The Owl and the Pussy-cat" —*Eugene Field*

The Owl and the Pussy-cat went to sea
In a beautiful pea-green boat,
They took some honey, and plenty of money,
Wrapped up in a five-pound note.

The Owl looked up to the stars above,
And sang to a small guitar,
"O lovely Pussy! O Pussy, my love,
What a beautiful Pussy you are,
You are,
You are!
What a beautiful Pussy you are!"

Pussy said to the Owl, "You elegant fowl!
How charmingly sweet you sing!
O let us be married! too long we have tarried:
But what shall we do for a ring?"

They sailed away, for a year and a day,
To the land where the Bong-Tree grows,
And there in a wood a Piggy-wig stood,
With a ring at the end of his nose,
His nose,
His nose,
With a ring at the end of his nose.

"Dear Pig, are you willing to sell for one shilling
Your ring?" Said the Piggy, "I will."
So they took it away, and were married next day
By the Turkey who lives on the hill.

They dined on mince, and slices of quince,
Which they ate with a runcible spoon;
And hand in hand, on the edge of the sand,
They danced by the light of the moon,
The moon,
The moon,
They danced by the light of the moon.

"My Cat and I" —*Aileen Fisher*

First lines: "When I flop down / to take a rest / my cat jumps up / upon my chest"

This poem can be found in the following:
  "Poetry Friday: A Poem by Aileen Fisher," at http://debbiediller.wordpress
  .com/2012/04/27/poetry-friday-a-poem-by-aileen-fisher.

"Speaking of Cows" —*Kaye Starbird*

First lines: "Speaking of cows (which no one was doing), / Why are they always staring and chewing?"

This poem can be found in the following:
  Starbird, Kaye. *Speaking of Cows and Other Poems.* Philadelphia: Lippincott,
  1960.

Topic: I Love You

"Somebody Loves You Deep and True" —*Anon.*

Somebody loves you deep and true.
If I weren't so bashful I'd tell you who.

"I Found a Silver Dollar" —*Dennis Lee*

First lines: "I found a silver dollar, / But I had to pay the rent"

This poem can be found in the following:
  Lee, Dennis. *Alligator Pie.* Illus. by Frank Newfeld. Boston: Houghton Mifflin, 1975.

"I Love You, I Love You" —*Anon.*

I love you, I love you,
I love you divine.
Please give me your bubble gum,
You're sitting on mine.

"Josephine, Josephine" —*Alexander Resnikoff*

First lines: "Josephine, Josephine, / The meanest girl I've ever seen"

This poem can be found in the following:
> Prelutsky, Jack, ed. *The Random House Book of Poetry for Children.* Illus. by Arnold Lobel. New York: Random House, 1983.

"I Saw a Little Girl I Hate" —*Arnold Spilka*

First lines: "I saw a little girl I hate / And kicked her with my toes"

This poem can be found in the following:
> Prelutsky, Jack, ed. *The Random House Book of Poetry for Children.* Illus. by Arnold Lobel. New York: Random House, 1983.

"Short Love Poem" —*Judith Viorst*

First lines: "It's hard to love / The tallest girl / When you're the shortest guy"

This poem can be found in the following:
> Viorst, Judith. *If I Were in Charge of the World: And Other Worries.* New York: Aladdin, 1981.

"Huckleberry, Gooseberry, Raspberry Pie" —*Clyde Watson*

First lines: "Huckleberry, gooseberry, raspberry pie / All sweetest things one cannot buy"

This poem can be found in the following:
> Prelutsky, Jack, ed. *The Random House Book of Poetry for Children.* Illus. by Arnold Lobel. New York: Random House, 1983.

Topic: Classics

"The Duel" —*Eugene Field*

The gingham dog and the calico cat
Side by side on the table sat;
'Twas half-past twelve, and (what do you think!)
Nor one nor t'other had slept a wink!

The old Dutch clock and the Chinese plate
Appeared to know as sure as fate
There was going to be a terrible spat.
(I wasn't there; I simply state
What was told to me by the Chinese plate!)

The gingham dog went "Bow-wow-wow!"
And the calico cat replied "Mee-ow!"
The air was littered, an hour or so,
With bits of gingham and calico,

While the old Dutch clock in the chimney-place
Up with its hands before its face,
For it always dreaded a family row!
(Now mind: I'm only telling you
What the old Dutch clock declares is true!)

The Chinese plate looked very blue,
And wailed, "Oh, dear! what shall we do!"
But the gingham dog and the calico cat
Wallowed this way and tumbled that,

Employing every tooth and claw
In the awfullest way you ever saw—
And, oh! How the gingham and calico flew!
(Don't fancy I exaggerate—
I got my news from the Chinese plate!)

Next morning, where the two had sat
They found no trace of dog or cat;
And some folks think unto this day
That burglars stole that pair away!

But the truth about the cat and pup
Is this: they ate each other up!
Now what do you really think of that!
(The old Dutch clock it told me so,
And that is how I came to know.)

"Casey at the Bat"   —*Ernest L. Thayer*

It looked extremely rocky for the Mudville nine that day;
The score stood two to four, with but an inning left to play.
So, when Cooney died at second, and Burrows did the same,
A pallor wreathed the features of the patrons of the game.

A straggling few got up to go, leaving there the rest,
With that hope which springs eternal within the human breast.
For they thought: "If only Casey could get a whack at that,"
They'd put even money now, with Casey at the bat.

But Flynn preceded Casey, and likewise so did Blake,
And the former was a pudd'n, and the latter was a fake.
So on that stricken multitude a deathlike silence sat;
For there seemed but little chance of Casey's getting to the bat.

But Flynn let drive a "single," to the wonderment of all.
And the much-despised Blakey "tore the cover off the ball."
And when the dust had lifted, and they saw what had occurred,
There was Blakey safe at second, and Flynn a-huggin' third.

Then from the gladdened multitude went up a joyous yell—
It rumbled in the mountaintops, it rattled in the dell;
It struck upon the hillside and rebounded on the flat;
For Casey, mighty Casey, was advancing to the bat.

There was ease in Casey's manner as he stepped into his place,
There was pride in Casey's bearing and a smile on Casey's face;
And when responding to the cheers he lightly doffed his hat,
No stranger in the crowd could doubt 'twas Casey at the bat.

Ten thousand eyes were on him as he rubbed his hands with dirt,
Five thousand tongues applauded when he wiped them on his shirt;
Then when the writhing pitcher ground the ball into his hip,
Defiance glanced in Casey's eye, a sneer curled Casey's lip.

And now the leather-covered sphere came hurtling through the air,
And Casey stood a-watching it in haughty grandeur there.
Close by the sturdy batsman the ball unheeded sped;
"That ain't my style," said Casey. "Strike one," the umpire said.

From the benches, black with people, there went up a muffled roar,
Like the beating of the storm waves on the stern and distant shore.
"Kill him! kill the umpire!" shouted someone on the stand;
And it's likely they'd have killed him had not Casey raised his hand.

With a smile of Christian charity great Casey's visage shone;
He stilled the rising tumult, he made the game go on;
He signaled to the pitcher, and once more the spheroid flew;
But Casey still ignored it, and the umpire said, "Strike two."

"Fraud!" cried the maddened thousands, and the echo answered "Fraud!"
But one scornful look from Casey and the audience was awed;
They saw his face grow stern and cold, they saw his muscles strain,
And they knew that Casey wouldn't let the ball go by again.

The sneer is gone from Casey's lips, his teeth are clenched in hate,
He pounds with cruel vengeance his bat upon the plate;

And now the pitcher holds the ball, and now he lets it go,
And now the air is shattered by the force of Casey's blow.

Oh, somewhere in this favored land the sun is shining bright,
The band is playing somewhere, and somewhere hearts are light;
And somewhere men are laughing, and somewhere children shout,
But there is no joy in Mudville: Mighty Casey has struck out.

This poem can be found in the following:

Thayer, Ernest Lawrence. *Casey at the Bat: A Ballad of the Republic Sung in the Year 1888.* Illus. by Christopher H. Bing. Brooklyn: Handprint, 2000.

"Jabberwocky" *—Lewis Carroll*

'Twas brillig, and the slithy toves
Did gyre and gimble in the wabe;
All mimsy were the borogoves,
And the mome raths outgrabe.

"Beware the Jabberwock, my son!
The jaws that bite, the claws that catch!
Beware the Jubjub bird, and shun
The frumious Bandersnatch!"

He took his vorpal sword in hand:
Long time the manxome foe he sought—
So rested he by the Tumtum tree,
And stood awhile in thought.

And as in uffish thought he stood,
The Jabberwock, with eyes of flame,
Came whiffling through the tulgey wood,
And burbled as it came!

One, two! One, two! And through and through
The vorpal blade went snicker-snack!
He left it dead, and with its head
He went galumphing back.

"And hast thou slain the Jabberwock!
Come to my arms, my beamish boy!
O frabjous day! Callooh! Callay!"
He chortled in his joy.

'Twas brillig, and the slithy toves
Did gyre and gimble in the wabe;
All mimsy were the borogoves,
And the mome raths outgrabe.

This poem can be found in the following:
Carroll, Lewis. *Through the Looking Glass and What Alice Found There.* New
York: Macmillan, 1871.

"Hiawatha's Childhood"   —*Henry Wadsworth Longfellow*

By the shores of Gitche Gumee,
By the shining Big-Sea-Water,
Stood Nokomis, the old woman,
Pointing with her finger westward,
O'er the water pointing westward,
To the purple clouds of sunset.
　　Fiercely the red sun descending
Burned his way along the heavens,
Set the sky on fire behind him,
As war-parties, when retreating,
Burn the prairies on their war-trail;
And the moon, the Night-sun, eastward,
Suddenly starting from his ambush,
Followed fast those bloody footprints,
Followed in that fiery war-trail,
With its glare upon his features.
　　And Nokomis, the old woman,
Pointing with her finger westward,
Spake these words to Hiawatha:
"Yonder dwells the great Pearl-Feather,
Megissogwon, the Magician,
Manito of Wealth and Wampum,
Guarded by his fiery serpents,
Guarded by the black pitch-water.
You can see his fiery serpents,
The Kenabeek, the great serpents,
Coiling, playing in the water;
You can see the black pitch-water
Stretching far away beyond them,
To the purple clouds of sunset!
　　"He it was who slew my father,
By his wicked wiles and cunning,

When he from the moon descended,
When he came on earth to seek me.
He, the mightiest of Magicians,
Sends the fever from the marshes,
Sends the pestilential vapors,
Sends the poisonous exhalations,
Sends the white fog from the fen-lands,
Sends disease and death among us!"
    "Take your bow, O Hiawatha,
Take your arrows, jasper-headed,
Take your war-club, Puggawaugun,
And your mittens, Minjekahwun,
And your birch-canoe for sailing,
And the oil of Mishe-Nahma,
So to smear its sides, that swiftly
You may pass the black pitch-water;
Slay this merciless magician,
Save the people from the fever
That he breathes across the fen-lands,
And avenge my father's murder!"
    Straightway then my Hiawatha
Armed himself with all his war-gear,
Launched his birch-canoe for sailing;
With his palm its sides he patted,
Said with glee, "Cheemaun, my darling,
O my Birch-canoe! leap forward,
Where you see the fiery serpents,
Where you see the black pitch-water!"
    Forward leaped Cheemaun exulting,
And the noble Hiawatha
Sang his war-song wild and woeful,
And above him the war-eagle,
The Keneu, the great war-eagle,
Master of all fowls with feathers,
Screamed and hurtled through the heavens.
    Soon he reached the fiery serpents,
The Kenabeek, the great serpents,
Lying huge upon the water,
Sparkling, rippling in the water,
Lying coiled across the passage,
With their blazing crests uplifted,

Breathing fiery fogs and vapors,
So that none could pass beyond them.
    But the fearless Hiawatha
Cried aloud, and spake in this wise:
"Let me pass my way, Kenabeek,
Let me go upon my journey!"
And they answered, hissing fiercely,
With their fiery breath made answer:
"Back, go back! O Shaugodaya!
Back to old Nokomis, Faint-heart!"
    Then the angry Hiawatha
Raised his mighty bow of ash-tree,
Seized his arrows, jasper-headed,
Shot them fast among the serpents;
Every twanging of the bow-string
Was a war-cry and a death-cry,
Every whizzing of an arrow
Was a death-song of Kenabeek.
    Weltering in the bloody water,
Dead lay all the fiery serpents,
And among them Hiawatha
Harmless sailed, and cried exulting:
"Onward, O Cheemaun, my darling!
Onward to the black pitch-water!"
    Then he took the oil of Nahma,
And the bows and sides anointed,
Smeared them well with oil, that swiftly
He might pass the black pitch-water.
All night long he sailed upon it,
Sailed upon that sluggish water,
Covered with its mould of ages,
Black with rotting water-rushes,
Rank with flags and leaves of lilies,
Stagnant, lifeless, dreary, dismal,
Lighted by the shimmering moonlight,
And by will-o'-the-wisps illumined,
Fires by ghosts of dead men kindled,
In their weary night-encampments.
    All the air was white with moonlight,
All the water black with shadow,
And around him the Suggema,

The mosquito, sang his war-song,
And the fire-flies, Wah-wah-taysee,
Waved their torches to mislead him;
And the bull-frog, the Dahinda,
Thrust his head into the moonlight,
Fixed his yellow eyes upon him,
Sobbed and sank beneath the surface;
And anon a thousand whistles,
Answered over all the fen-lands,
And the heron, the Shuh-shuh-gah,
Far off on the reedy margin,
Heralded the hero's coming.
    Westward thus fared Hiawatha,
Toward the realm of Megissogwon,
Toward the land of the Pearl-Feather,
Till the level moon stared at him,
In his face stared pale and haggard,
Till the sun was hot behind him,
Till it burned upon his shoulders,
And before him on the upland
He could see the Shining Wigwam
Of the Manito of Wampum,
Of the mightiest of Magicians.
    Then once more Cheemaun he patted,
To his birch-canoe said, "Onward!"
And it stirred in all its fibres,
And with one great bound of triumph
Leaped across the water-lilies,
Leaped through tangled flags and rushes,
And upon the beach beyond them
Dry-shod landed Hiawatha.
    Straight he took his bow of ash-tree,
On the sand one end he rested,
With his knee he pressed the middle,
Stretched the faithful bow-string tighter,
Took an arrow, jasper-headed,
Shot it at the Shining Wigwam,
Sent it singing as a herald,
As a bearer of his message,
Of his challenge loud and lofty:
"Come forth from your lodge, Pearl-Feather!
Hiawatha waits your coming!"

Straightway from the Shining Wigwam
Came the mighty Megissogwon,
Tall of stature, broad of shoulder,
Dark and terrible in aspect,
Clad from head to foot in wampum,
Armed with all his warlike weapons,
Painted like the sky of morning,
Streaked with crimson, blue, and yellow,
Crested with great eagle-feathers,
Streaming upward, streaming outward.
  "Well I know you, Hiawatha!"
Cried he in a voice of thunder,
In a tone of loud derision.
"Hasten back, O Shaugodaya!
Hasten back among the women,
Back to old Nokomis, Faint-heart!
I will slay you as you stand there,
As of old I slew her father!"
  But my Hiawatha answered,
Nothing daunted, fearing nothing:
"Big words do not smite like war-clubs,
Boastful breath is not a bow-string,
Taunts are not so sharp as arrows,
Deeds are better things than words are,
Actions mightier than boastings!"
  Then began the greatest battle
That the sun had ever looked on,
That the war-birds ever witnessed.
All a Summer's day it lasted,
From the sunrise to the sunset;
For the shafts of Hiawatha
Harmless hit the shirt of wampum,
Harmless fell the blows he dealt it
With his mittens, Minjekahwun,
Harmless fell the heavy war-club;
It could dash the rocks asunder,
But it could not break the meshes
Of that magic shirt of wampum.
  Till at sunset Hiawatha,
Leaning on his bow of ash-tree,
Wounded, weary, and desponding,
With his mighty war-club broken,

With his mittens torn and tattered,
And three useless arrows only,
Paused to rest beneath a pine-tree,
From whose branches trailed the mosses,
And whose trunk was coated over
With the Dead-man's Moccasin-leather,
With the fungus white and yellow.
  Suddenly from the boughs above him
Sang the Mama, the woodpecker:
"Aim your arrows, Hiawatha,
At the head of Megissogwon,
Strike the tuft of hair upon it,
At their roots the long black tresses;
There alone can he be wounded!"
  Winged with feathers, tipped with jasper,
Swift flew Hiawatha's arrow,
Just as Megissogwon, stooping,
Raised a heavy stone to throw it.
Full upon the crown it struck him,
At the roots of his long tresses,
And he reeled and staggered forward,
Plunging like a wounded bison,
Yes, like Pezhekee, the bison,
When the snow is on the prairie.
  Swifter flew the second arrow,
In the pathway of the other,
Piercing deeper than the other,
Wounding sorer than the other;
And the knees of Megissogwon
Shook like windy reeds beneath him,
Bent and trembled like the rushes.
  But the third and latest arrow
Swiftest flew, and wounded sorest,
And the mighty Megissogwon
Saw the fiery eyes of Pauguk,
Saw the eyes of Death glare at him,
Heard his voice call in the darkness;
At the feet of Hiawatha
Lifeless lay the great Pearl-Feather,
Lay the mightiest of Magicians.
  Then the grateful Hiawatha
Called the Mama, the woodpecker,

From his perch among the branches
Of the melancholy pine-tree,
And, in honor of his service,
Stained with blood the tuft of feathers
On the little head of Mama;
Even to this day he wears it,
Wears the tuft of crimson feathers,
As a symbol of his service.

Then he stripped the shirt of wampum
From the back of Megissogwon,
As a trophy of the battle,
As a signal of his conquest.
On the shore he left the body,
Half on land and half in water,
In the sand his feet were buried,
And his face was in the water.
And above him, wheeled and clamored
The Keneu, the great war-eagle,
Sailing round in narrower circles,
Hovering nearer, nearer, nearer.

From the wigwam Hiawatha
Bore the wealth of Megissogwon,
All his wealth of skins and wampum,
Furs of bison and of beaver,
Furs of sable and of ermine,
Wampum belts and strings and pouches,
Quivers wrought with beads of wampum,
Filled with arrows, silver-headed.

Homeward then he sailed exulting,
Homeward through the black pitch-water,
Homeward through the weltering serpents,
With the trophies of the battle,
With a shout and song of triumph.

On the shore stood old Nokomis,
On the shore stood Chibiabos,
And the very strong man, Kwasind,
Waiting for the hero's coming,
Listening to his songs of triumph.
And the people of the village
Welcomed him with songs and dances,
Made a joyous feast, and shouted:
"Honor be to Hiawatha!

He has slain the great Pearl-Feather,
Slain the mightiest of Magicians,
Him, who sent the fiery fever,
Sent the white fog from the fen-lands,
Sent disease and death among us!"
   Ever dear to Hiawatha
Was the memory of Mama!
And in token of his friendship,
As a mark of his remembrance,
He adorned and decked his pipe-stem
With the crimson tuft of feathers,
With the blood-red crest of Mama.
But the wealth of Megissogwon,
All the trophies of the battle,
He divided with his people,
Shared it equally among them.

This poem can be found in the following:

Longfellow, Henry Wadsworth. *The Complete Poetical Works of Henry Wadsworth Longfellow.* Boston: Houghton, Mifflin, 1893.

Longfellow, Henry Wadsworth. *Hiawatha.* Illus. by Susan Jeffers. New York: Dial Books for Young Readers, 1983.

"Paul Revere's Ride"   *—Henry Wadsworth Longfellow*

Listen, my children, and you shall hear
Of the midnight ride of Paul Revere,
On the eighteenth of April, in Seventy-five;
Hardly a man is now alive
Who remembers that famous day and year.

He said to his friend, "If the British march
By land or sea from the town tonight,
Hang a lantern aloft in the belfry arch
Of the North Church tower as a signal light,—
One, if by land, and two, if by sea;
And I on the opposite shore will be,
Ready to ride and spread the alarm
Through every Middlesex village and farm,
For the country folk to be up and to arm."

Then he said, "Good-night!" and with muffled oar
Silently rowed to the Charlestown shore,

Just as the moon rose over the bay,
Where swinging wide at her moorings lay
The Somerset, British man-of-war;
A phantom ship, with each mast and spar
Across the moon like a prison bar,
And a huge black hulk, that was magnified
By its own reflection in the tide

Meanwhile, his friend, through alley and street,
Wanders and watches with eager ears,
Till in the silence around him he hears
The muster of men at the barrack door,
The sound of arms, and the tramp of feet,
And the measured tread of the grenadiers,
Marching down to their boats on the shore.

Then he climbed the tower of the Old North Church,
By the wooden stairs, with stealthy tread,
To the belfry-chamber overhead,
And startled the pigeons from their perch
On the sombre rafters, that round him made
Masses and moving shapes of shade,—
By the trembling ladder, steep and tall,
To the highest window in the wall,
Where he paused to listen and look down
A moment on the roofs of the town,
And the moonlight flowing over all

Beneath, in the churchyard, lay the dead,
In their night-encampment on the hill,
Wrapped in silence so deep and still
That he could hear, like a sentinel's tread,
The watchful night-wind, as it went
Creeping along from tent to tent,
And seeming to whisper, "All is well!"
A moment only he feels the spell
Of the place and the hour, and the secret dread
Of the lonely belfry and the dead;
For suddenly all his thoughts are bent
On a shadowy something far away,
Where the river widens to meet the bay,—
A line of black that bends and floats
On the rising tide, like a bridge of boats.

Meanwhile, impatient to mount and ride,
Booted and spurred, with a heavy stride
On the opposite shore walked Paul Revere.
Now he patted his horse's side,
Now gazed at the landscape far and near,
Then, impetuous, stamped the earth,
And turned and tightened his saddle-girth;
But mostly he watched with eager search
The belfry-tower of the Old North Church,
As it rose above the graves on the hill,
Lonely and spectral and sombre and still
And lo! as he looks, on the belfry's height
A glimmer, and then a gleam of light!
He springs to the saddle, the bridle he turns,
But lingers and gazes, till full on his sight
A second lamp in the belfry burns!

A hurry of hoofs in a village street,
A shape in the moonlight, a bulk in the dark,
And beneath, from the pebbles, in passing, a spark
Struck out by a steed flying fearless and fleet:
That was all! And yet, through the gloom and the light,
The fate of a nation was riding that night;
And the spark struck out by that steed, in his flight,
Kindled the land into flame with its heat.
He has left the village and mounted the steep,
And beneath him, tranquil and broad and deep,
Is the Mystic, meeting the ocean tides;
And under the alders that skirt its edge,
Now soft on the sand, now loud on the ledge,
Is heard the tramp of his steed as he rides.

It was twelve by the village clock,
When he crossed the bridge into Medford town.
He heard the crowing of the cock,
And the barking of the farmer's dog,
And felt the damp of the river fog
That rises after the sun goes down

It was one by the village clock,
When he galloped into Lexington.
He saw the gilded weathercock

Swim in the moonlight as he passed,
And the meeting-house windows blank and bare,
Gaze at him with a spectral glare,
As if they already stood aghast
At the bloody work they would look upon.

It was two by the village clock,
When he came to the bridge in Concord town.
He heard the bleating of the flock,
And the twitter of birds among the trees,
And felt the breath of the morning breeze
Blowing over the meadows brown.
And one was safe and asleep in his bed
Who at the bridge would be first to fall,
Who that day would be lying dead,
Pierced by a British musket-ball.

You know the rest. In the books you have read,
How the British Regulars fired and fled,—
How the farmers gave them ball for ball,
From behind each fence and farmyard wall,
Chasing the red-coats down the lane,
Then crossing the fields to emerge again
Under the trees at the turn of the road,
And only pausing to fire and load
So through the night rode Paul Revere;
And so through the night went his cry of alarm
To every Middlesex village and farm,—
A cry of defiance and not of fear,
A voice in the darkness, a knock at the door,
And a word that shall echo forever-more!
For, borne on the night-wind of the Past,
Through all our history, to the last,
In the hour of darkness and peril and need,
The people will waken and listen to hear
The hurrying hoof-beats of that steed,
And the midnight message of Paul Revere.

This poem can be found in the following:
Longfellow, Henry Wadsworth. *The Complete Poetical Works of Henry Wadsworth Longfellow.* Boston: Houghton, Mifflin, 1893.
Longfellow, Henry Wadsworth. *The Midnight Ride of Paul Revere.* Illus. by Christopher H. Bing. Brooklyn: Handprint, 2001.

"Lincoln"
—Nancy Byrd Turner

There was a boy of other days,
A quiet, awkward, earnest lad,
Who trudged long weary miles to get
A book on which his heart was set—
And then no candle had!

He was too poor to buy a lamp
But very wise in woodmen's ways.
He gathered seasoned bough and stem,
And crisping leaf, and kindled them
Into a ruddy blaze.

Then as he lay full length and read,
The firelight flickered on his face,
And etched his shadow on the gloom,
And made a picture in the room,
In that most humble place.

The hard years came, the hard years went,
But, gentle, brave, and strong of will,
He met them all. And when today
We see his pictured face, we say,
"There's light upon it still."

This poem can be found in the following:

Arbuthnot, May Hill, and Shelton L. Root, eds. *Time for Poetry: A Representative Collection of Poetry for Children, to Be Used in the Classroom, Home, or Camp; Especially Planned for College Classes in Children's Literature.* Illus. by Arthur Paul. Glenview, IL: Scott, Foresman, 1967.

Ferris, Helen Josephine. *Favorite Poems: Old and New.* Illus. by Leonard Weisgard. Garden City, NY: Doubleday, 1957.

Prelutsky, Jack, ed. *The Random House Book of Poetry for Children.* Illus. by Arnold Lobel. New York: Random House, 1983.

"America for Me"
—Henry Van Dyke

'Tis fine to see the Old World and travel up and down
Among the famous palaces and cities of renown,
To admire the crumbling castles and the statues and kings
But now I think I've had enough of antiquated things.

So it's home again, and home again, America for me!
My heart is turning home again and there I long to be,

In the land of youth and freedom, beyond the ocean bars,
Where the air is full of sunlight and the flag is full of stars.

Oh, London is a man's town, there's power in the air;
And Paris is a woman's town, with flowers in her hair;
And it's sweet to dream in Venice, and it's great to study Rome;
But when it comes to living there is no place like home.

I like the German fir-woods in green battalions drilled;
I like the gardens of Versailles with flashing fountains filled;
But, oh, to take your hand, my dear, and ramble for a day
In the friendly western woodland where Nature has her sway!

I know that Europe's wonderful, yet something seems to lack!
The Past is too much with her, and the people looking back.
But the glory of the Present is to make the Future free—
We love our land for what she is and what she is to be.

Oh, it's home again, and home again, America for me!
I want a ship that's westward bound to plough the rolling sea,
To the blessed Land of Room Enough, beyond the ocean bars,
Where the air is full of sunlight and the flag is full of stars.

This poem can be found in the following:

Felleman, Hazel, ed. *The Best Loved Poems of the American People.* New York: Doubleday, 1990.

Perrine, Laurence. *Sound and Sense, an Introduction to Poetry.* New York: Harcourt, Brace and World, 1963.

Sword, Elizabeth Hauge, and Victoria McCarthy, eds. *A Child's Anthology of Poetry.* Illus. by Tom Pohrt. Hopewell, NJ: Ecco, 1995.

"If"   —*Rudyard Kipling*

If you can keep your head when all about you
Are losing theirs and blaming it on you,
If you can trust yourself when all men doubt you,
But make allowance for their doubting too;

If you can wait and not be tired by waiting,
Or being lied about, don't deal in lies,
Or being hated, don't give way to hating,
And yet don't look too good, nor talk too wise:

If you can dream—and not make dreams your master;
If you can think—and not make thoughts your aim;

If you can meet with Triumph and Disaster
And treat those two impostors just the same;

If you can bear to hear the truth you've spoken
Twisted by knaves to make a trap for fools,
Or watch the things you gave your life to, broken,
And stoop and build 'em up with worn-out tools:

If you can make one heap of all your winnings
And risk it on one turn of pitch-and-toss,
And lose, and start again at your beginnings
And never breathe a word about your loss;

If you can force your heart and nerve and sinew
To serve your turn long after they are gone,
And so hold on when there is nothing in you
Except the Will which says to them: "Hold on!"

If you can talk with crowds and keep your virtue,
Or walk with Kings—nor lose the common touch,
If neither foes nor loving friends can hurt you,
If all men count with you, but none too much;

If you can fill the unforgiving minute
With sixty seconds' worth of distance run,
Yours is the Earth and everything that's in it,
And—which is more—you'll be a Man, my son!

This poem can be found in the following:
> Doan, Eleanor Lloyd. *A Child's Treasury of Verse.* Illus. by Nancy Munger.
> Grand Rapids: Zondervan, 1977.
> Sword, Elizabeth Hauge, and Victoria McCarthy, eds. *A Child's Anthology of
> Poetry.* Illus. by Tom Pohrt. Hopewell, NJ: Ecco, 1995.

"Solitude"   —*Ella Wheeler Wilcox*

Laugh, and the world laughs with you;
Weep, and you weep alone;
For the sad old earth must borrow its mirth,
But has trouble enough of its own.

Sing, and the hills will answer;
Sigh, it is lost on the air;
The echoes bound to a joyful sound,
But shrink from voicing care.

Rejoice, and men will seek you;
Grieve, and they turn and go;
They want full measure of all your pleasure,
But they do not need your woe.

Be glad, and your friends are many;
Be sad, and you lose them all,—
There are none to decline your nectared wine,
But alone you must drink life's gall.

Feast, and your halls are crowded;
Fast, and the world goes by.
Succeed and give, and it helps you live,
But no man can help you die.

There is room in the halls of pleasure
For a large and lordly train,
But one by one we must all file on
Through the narrow aisles of pain.

"A Cradle Hymn"

—*Isaac Watts*

Hush! my dear, lie still and slumber,
Holy angels guard thy bed!
Heavenly blessings without number
Gently falling on thy head.

Sleep, my babe; thy food and raiment,
House and home, thy friends provide;
All without thy care or payment:
All thy wants are well supplied.

How much better thou'rt attended
Than the Son of God could be,
When from heaven He descended
And became a child like thee!

Soft and easy is thy cradle:
Coarse and hard thy Saviour lay,
When His birthplace was a stable
And His softest bed was hay.

Blessèd babe! what glorious features—
Spotless fair, divinely bright!
Must He dwell with brutal creatures?
How could angels bear the sight?

Was there nothing but a manger
Cursèd sinners could afford
To receive the heavenly stranger?
Did they thus affront their Lord?

Soft, my child: I did not chide thee,
Though my song might sound too hard;
'Tis thy mother sits beside thee,
And her arms shall be thy guard.

Yet to read the shameful story
How the Jews abused their King,
How they served the Lord of Glory,
Makes me angry while I sing.

See the kinder shepherds round Him,
Telling wonders from the sky!
Where they sought Him, there they found Him,
With His Virgin mother by.

See the lovely babe a-dressing;
Lovely infant, how He smiled!
When He wept, the mother's blessing
Soothed and hush'd the holy child.

Lo, He slumbers in His manger,
Where the hornèd oxen fed:
Peace, my darling; here's no danger,
Here's no ox anear thy bed.

'Twas to save thee, child, from dying,
Save my dear from burning flame,
Bitter groans and endless crying,
That thy blest Redeemer came.

May'st thou live to know and fear Him,
Trust and love Him all thy days;
Then go dwell for ever near Him,
See His face, and sing His praise!

"In Flanders Field" —John McCrae

In Flanders fields the poppies blow
Between the crosses, row on row,
That mark our place; and in the sky
The larks, still bravely singing, fly
Scarce heard amid the guns below.

We are the Dead. Short days ago
We lived, felt dawn, saw sunset glow,
Loved and were loved, and now we lie
In Flanders fields.

Take up our quarrel with the foe:
To you from failing hands we throw
The torch; be yours to hold it high.
If ye break faith with us who die
We shall not sleep, though poppies grow
In Flanders fields.

"The Flag Goes By" —Henry Holcomb Bennett

Hats off!
Along the street there comes
A blare of bugles, a ruffle of drums,
A dash of color beneath the sky:
Hats off!
The flag is passing by!

Blue and crimson and white it shines,
Over the steel-tipped, ordered lines.
Hats off!
The colors before us fly;
But more than the flag is passing by.

Sea-fights and land-fights, grim and great,
Fought to make and to save the State:
Weary marches and sinking ships;
Cheers of victory on dying lips;

Days of plenty and years of peace;
March of a strong land's swift increase;
Equal justice, right and law,
Stately honor and reverend awe;

Sign of a nation, great and strong
To ward her people from foreign wrong:
Pride and glory and honor,—all
Live in the colors to stand or fall.

Hats off!
Along the street there comes
A blare of bugles, a ruffle of drums;
And loyal hearts are beating high:
Hats off!
The flag is passing by!

Psalm 23

The Lord is my shepherd; I shall not want.
He maketh me to lie down in green pastures:
    he leadeth me beside the still waters.
He restoreth my soul: he leadeth me in the paths
    of righteousness for his name's sake.
Yea, though I walk through the valley of the shadow of death,
    I will fear no evil: for thou art with me;
    thy rod and thy staff they comfort me.
Thou preparest a table before me in the presence of mine enemies:
    thou anointest my head with oil; my cup runneth over.
Surely goodness and mercy shall follow me all the days of my life:
    and I will dwell in the house of the Lord for ever.

"A Lullaby"

—Lewis Carroll

Speak roughly to your little boy,
And beat him when he sneezes:
He only does it to annoy,
Because he knows it teases.
Wow! wow! wow!

I speak severely to my boy,
I beat him when he sneezes;
For he can thoroughly enjoy
The pepper when he pleases!
Wow! wow! wow!

"Red Queen's Lullaby" —*Lewis Carroll*

Hush-a-by lady, in Alice's lap!
Till the feast's ready, we've time for a nap:
When the feast's over, we'll go to the ball—
Red Queen, and White Queen, and Alice, and all!

"Abou Ben Adhem" —*Leigh Hunt*

(variant title "Abou Ben Adhem and the Angel")

Abou Ben Adhem (may his tribe increase!)
Awoke one night from a deep dream of peace,
And saw, within the moonlight in his room,
Making it rich, and like a lily in bloom,
An Angel writing in a book of gold:
Exceeding peace had made Ben Adhem bold,
And to the Presence in the room he said,
"What writest thou?" The Vision raised its head,
And with a look made of all sweet accord
Answered, "The names of those who love the Lord."
"And is mine one?" said Abou. "Nay, not so,"
Replied the Angel. Abou spoke more low,
But cheerly still; and said, "I pray thee, then,
Write me as one that loves his fellow-men."

The Angel wrote, and vanished. The next night
It came again with a great wakening light,
And showed the names whom love of God had blessed,
And, lo! Ben Adhem's name led all the rest!

"Charge of the Light Brigade" —*Alfred Tennyson*

I
Half a league, half a league,
Half a league onward,
All in the valley of Death
Rode the six hundred.
"Forward, the Light Brigade!
Charge for the guns!" he said.
Into the valley of Death
Rode the six hundred.

II
"Forward, the Light Brigade!"
Was there a man dismayed?
Not though the soldier knew
Someone had blundered.
Theirs not to make reply,
Theirs not to reason why,
Theirs but to do and die.
Into the valley of Death
Rode the six hundred.

III
Cannon to right of them,
Cannon to left of them,
Cannon in front of them
Volleyed and thundered;
Stormed at with shot and shell,
Boldly they rode and well,
Into the jaws of Death,
Into the mouth of hell
Rode the six hundred.

IV
Flashed all their sabres bare,
Flashed as they turned in air
Sabring the gunners there,
Charging an army, while
All the world wondered.
Plunged in the battery-smoke
Right through the line they broke;
Cossack and Russian
Reeled from the sabre stroke
Shattered and sundered.
Then they rode back, but not
Not the six hundred.

V
Cannon to right of them,
Cannon to left of them,
Cannon behind them
Volleyed and thundered;
Stormed at with shot and shell,
While horse and hero fell.

They that had fought so well
Came through the jaws of Death,
Back from the mouth of hell,
All that was left of them,
Left of six hundred.

VI
When can their glory fade?
O the wild charge they made!
All the world wondered.
Honour the charge they made!
Honour the Light Brigade,
Noble six hundred!

"Grass" —*Carl Sandburg*

Pile the bodies high at Austerlitz and Waterloo.
Shovel them under and let me work—
    I am the grass; I cover all.

And pile them high at Gettysburg
And pile them high at Ypres and Verdun.
Shovel them under and let me work.
Two years, ten years, and passengers ask the conductor:
    What place is this?
    Where are we now?

    I am the grass.
    Let me work.

"The Highwayman" —*Alfred Noyes*

The wind was a torrent of darkness among the gusty trees,
The moon was a ghostly galleon tossed upon cloudy seas,
The road was a ribbon of moonlight over the purple moor,
And the highwayman came riding—
    Riding—riding—
The highwayman came riding, up to the old inn-door.

He'd a French cocked-hat on his forehead, a bunch of lace at his chin,
A coat of the claret velvet, and breeches of brown doe-skin;
They fitted with never a wrinkle: his boots were up to the thigh.

And he rode with a jeweled twinkle,
   His pistol butts a-twinkle,
His rapier hilt a-twinkle, under the jeweled sky.

Over the cobbles he clattered and clashed in the dark inn-yard,
He tapped with his whip on the shutters, but all was locked and barred;
He whistled a tune to the window, and who should be waiting there
But the landlord's black-eyed daughter,
   Bess, the landlord's daughter,
Plaiting a dark red love-knot into her long black hair.

And dark in the dark old inn-yard a stable-wicket creaked
Where Tim the ostler listened; his face was white and peaked;
His eyes were hollows of madness, his hair like moldy hay,
But he loved the landlord's daughter,
   The landlord's red-lipped daughter,
Dumb as a dog he listened, and he heard the robber say—

"One kiss, my bonny sweetheart, I'm after a prize tonight,
But I shall be back with the yellow gold before the morning light;
Yet, if they press me sharply, and harry me through the day,
Then look for me by moonlight,
   Watch for me by moonlight,
I'll come to thee by moonlight, though hell should bar the way."

He rose upright in the stirrups; he scarce could reach her hand,
But she loosened her hair in the casement. His face burnt like a brand
As the black cascade of perfume came tumbling over his breast;
And he kissed its waves in the moonlight,
   (Oh, sweet black waves in the moonlight!)
Then he tugged at his rein in the moonlight, and galloped away to the West.

He did not come in the dawning; he did not come at noon;
And out of the tawny sunset, before the rise of the moon,
When the road was a gypsy's ribbon, looping the purple moor,
A red-coat troop came marching—
   Marching—marching—
King George's men came marching, up to the old inn-door.

They said no word to the landlord, they drank his ale instead,
But they gagged his daughter and bound her to the foot of her narrow bed;
Two of them knelt at her casement, with muskets at their side.
There was death at every window;
   And hell at one dark window;
For Bess could see, through her casement, the road that he would ride.

They had tied her up to attention, with many a sniggering jest.
They had bound a musket beside her, with the barrel beneath her breast.
"Now keep good watch!" and they kissed her. She heard the doomed man
    say—
Look for me by moonlight;
    Watch for me by moonlight;
I'll come to thee by moonlight, though hell should bar the way!

She twisted her hands behind her; but all the knots held good.
She writhed her hands till her fingers were wet with sweat or blood.
They stretched and strained in the darkness, and the hours crawled by like
    years,
Till, now, on the stroke of midnight,
    Cold, on the stroke of midnight,
The tip of one finger touched it! The trigger at least was hers!

The tip of one finger touched it. She strove no more for the rest.
Up, she stood up to attention, with the muzzle beneath her breast.
She would not risk their hearing; she would not strive again;
For the road lay bare in the moonlight;
    Blank and bare in the moonlight;
And the blood of her veins, in the moonlight, throbbed to her love's
    refrain.

Tlot-tlot; tlot-tlot! Had they heard it? The horse-hoofs ringing clear;
Tlot-tlot, tlot-tlot, in the distance? Were they deaf that they did not hear?
Down the ribbon of moonlight, over the brow of the hill,
The highwayman came riding,
    Riding, riding!
The red-coats looked to their priming! She stood up, straight and still!

Tlot-tlot, in the frosty silence! *Tlot-tlot,* in the echoing night!
Nearer he came and nearer! Her face was like a light!
Her eyes grew wide for a moment; she drew one last deep breath,
Then her finger moved in the moonlight,
    Her musket shattered the moonlight,
Shattered her breast in the moonlight and warned him—with her death.

He turned; he spurred to the west; he did not know who stood
Bowed, with her head o'er the musket, drenched with her own red blood.
Not till the dawn he heard it, his face grew gray to hear
How Bess, the landlord's daughter,
    The landlord's black-eyed daughter,
Had watched for her love in the moonlight, and died in the darkness there.

Back, he spurred like a madman, shouting a curse to the sky,
With the white road smoking behind him and his rapier brandished high!
Blood-red were his spurs in the golden noon; wine-red was his velvet coat,
When they shot him down on the highway,
    Down like a dog on the highway,
And he lay in his blood on the highway, with the bunch of lace at his
    throat.

And still of a winter's night, they say, when the wind is in the trees,
When the moon is a ghostly galleon tossed upon cloudy seas,
When the road is a ribbon of moonlight over the purple moor,
A highwayman comes riding—
    Riding—riding—
A highwayman comes riding, up to the old inn-door.

Over the cobbles he clatters and clangs in the dark inn-yard;
He taps with his whip on the shutters, but all is locked and barred;
He whistles a tune to the window, and who should be waiting there
But the landlord's black-eyed daughter,
    Bess, the landlord's daughter,
Plaiting a dark red love-knot into her long black hair.

From "Ode on Intimations of Immortality" —*William Wordsworth*

There was a time when meadow, grove, and stream,
The earth, and every common sight
To me did seem
Apparelled in celestial light,
The glory and the freshness of a dream.
It is not now as it hath been of yore;—
Turn wheresoe'er I may,
By night or day,
The things which I have seen I now can see no more.

The rainbow comes and goes,
And lovely is the rose;
The moon doth with delight
Look round her when the heavens are bare;
Waters on a starry night
Are beautiful and fair;
The sunshine is a glorious birth;
But yet I know, where'er I go,
That there hath past away a glory from the earth.

Now, while the birds thus sing a joyous song,
And while the young lambs bound
As to the tabor's sound,
To me alone there came a thought of grief:
A timely utterance gave that thought relief,
And I again am strong.
The cataracts blow their trumpets from the steep,—
No more shall grief of mine the season wrong:
I hear the echoes through the mountains throng.
The winds come to me from the fields of sleep,
And all the earth is gay;
Land and sea
Give themselves up to jollity,
And with the heart of May
Doth every beast keep holiday;—
Thou child of joy,
Shout round me, let me hear thy shouts, thou happy
Shepherd-boy!

Ye blessèd Creatures, I have heard the call
Ye to each other make; I see
The heavens laugh with you in your jubilee;
My heart is at your festival,
My head hath its coronal,
The fulness of your bliss, I feel—I feel it all.
O evil day! if I were sullen
While Earth herself is adorning
This sweet May-morning;
And the children are culling
On every side
In a thousand valleys far and wide
Fresh flowers; while the sun shines warm,
And the babe leaps up on his mother's arm:—
I hear, I hear, with joy I hear!
—But there's a tree, of many, one,
A single field which I have look'd upon,
Both of them speak of something that is gone:
The pansy at my feet
Doth the same tale repeat:
Whither is fled the visionary gleam?
Where is it now, the glory and the dream?

Our birth is but a sleep and a forgetting;
The Soul that rises with us, our life's Star,
Hath had elsewhere its setting
And cometh from afar;
Not in entire forgetfulness,
And not in utter nakedness,
But trailing clouds of glory do we come
From God, who is our home:
Heaven lies about us in our infancy!
Shades of the prison-house begin to close
Upon the growing Boy,
But he beholds the light, and whence it flows,
He sees it in his joy;
The Youth, who daily farther from the east
Must travel, still is Nature's priest,
And by the vision splendid
Is on his way attended;
At length the Man perceives it die away,
And fade into the light of common day.

Earth fills her lap with pleasures of her own;
Yearnings she hath in her own natural kind,
And, even with something of a mother's mind,
And no unworthy aim,
The homely nurse doth all she can
To make her foster-child, her inmate, Man,
Forget the glories he hath known,
And that imperial palace whence he came.

Behold the Child among his new-born blisses,
A six years' darling of a pigmy size!
See, where 'mid work of his own hand he lies,
Fretted by sallies of his mother's kisses,
With light upon him from his father's eyes!
See, at his feet, some little plan or chart,
Some fragment from his dream of human life,
Shaped by himself with newly-learned art;
A wedding or a festival,
A mourning or a funeral;
And this hath now his heart,
And unto this he frames his song:
Then will he fit his tongue

To dialogues of business, love, or strife;
But it will not be long
Ere this be thrown aside,
And with new joy and pride
The little actor cons another part;
Filling from time to time his "humorous stage"
With all the Persons, down to palsied Age,
That life brings with her in her equipage;
As if his whole vocation
Were endless imitation.

Thou, whose exterior semblance doth belie
Thy soul's immensity;
Thou best philosopher, who yet dost keep
Thy heritage, thou eye among the blind,
That, deaf and silent, read'st the eternal deep,
Haunted for ever by the eternal Mind,—
Mighty Prophet! Seer blest!
On whom those truths rest
Which we are toiling all our lives to find,
In darkness lost, the darkness of the grave;
Thou, over whom thy Immortality
Broods like the day, a master o'er a slave,
A Presence which is not to be put by;
To whom the grave
Is but a lonely bed, without the sense of sight
Of day or the warm light,
A place of thoughts where we in waiting lie;
Thou little child, yet glorious in the might
Of heaven-born freedom on thy being's height,
Why with such earnest pains dost thou provoke
The years to bring the inevitable yoke,
Thus blindly with thy blessedness at strife?
Full soon thy soul shall have her earthly freight,
And custom lie upon thee with a weight
Heavy as frost, and deep almost as life!

O joy! that in our embers
Is something that doth live,
That Nature yet remembers
What was so fugitive!
The thought of our past years in me doth breed

Perpetual benediction: not indeed
For that which is most worthy to be blest,
Delight and liberty, the simple creed
Of Childhood, whether busy or at rest,
With new-fledged hope still fluttering in his breast:—
—Not for these I raise
The song of thanks and praise;
But for those obstinate questionings
Of sense and outward things,
Fallings from us, vanishings,
Blank misgivings of a creature
Moving about in worlds not realized,
High instincts, before which our mortal nature
Did tremble like a guilty thing surprised:
But for those first affections,
Those shadowy recollections,
Which, be they what they may,
Are yet the fountain-light of all our day,
Are yet a master-light of all our seeing;
Uphold us—cherish—and have power to make
Our noisy years seem moments in the being
Of the eternal Silence: truths that wake,
To perish never;
Which neither listlessness, nor mad endeavour,
Nor man nor boy,
Nor all that is at enmity with joy,
Can utterly abolish or destroy!
Hence, in a season of calm weather
Though inland far we be,
Our souls have sight of that immortal sea
Which brought us hither;
Can in a moment travel thither—
And see the children sport upon the shore,
And hear the mighty waters rolling evermore.

Then, sing, ye birds, sing, sing a joyous song!
And let the young lambs bound
As to the tabor's sound!
We, in thought, will join your throng,
Ye that pipe and ye that play,
Ye that through your hearts to-day
Feel the gladness of the May!

What though the radiance which was once so bright
Be now for ever taken from my sight,
Though nothing can bring back the hour
Of splendour in the grass, of glory in the flower;
We will grieve not, rather find
Strength in what remains behind;
In the primal sympathy
Which having been must ever be;
In the soothing thoughts that spring
Out of human suffering;
In the faith that looks through death,
In years that bring the philosophic mind.

And O, ye Fountains, Meadows, Hills, and Groves,
Forebode not any severing of our loves!
Yet in my heart of hearts I feel your might;
I only have relinquish'd one delight
To live beneath your more habitual sway;
I love the brooks which down their channels fret
Even more than when I tripp'd lightly as they;
The innocent brightness of a new-born day
Is lovely yet;
The clouds that gather round the setting sun
Do take a sober colouring from an eye
That hath kept watch o'er man's mortality;
Another race hath been, and other palms are won.
Thanks to the human heart by which we live,
Thanks to its tenderness, its joys, and fears,
To me the meanest flower that blows can give
Thoughts that do often lie too deep for tears.

Psalm 24

The earth is the Lord's, and the fulness thereof;
    the world, and they that dwell therein.
For he hath founded it upon the seas, and established it upon the floods.
Who shall ascend into the hill of the Lord?
    or who shall stand in his holy place?
He that hath clean hands, and a pure heart;
    who hath not lifted up his soul unto vanity, nor sworn deceitfully.
He shall receive the blessing from the Lord,
    and righteousness from the God of his salvation.

This is the generation of them that seek him,
  that seek thy face, O Jacob. Selah.
Lift up your heads, O ye gates; and be ye lift up,
  ye everlasting doors; and the King of glory shall come in.
Who is this King of glory? The Lord strong and mighty,
  the Lord mighty in battle.
Lift up your heads, O ye gates; even lift them up,
  ye everlasting doors; and the King of glory shall come in.
Who is this King of glory? The Lord of hosts, he is the King of glory. Selah.

Scottish or Irish Blessing on Parting:

"Our joy was that we knew thee the days."

Topic: Food

"Through the Teeth"   *—Anon.*
  Through the teeth
  And past the gums
  Look out, stomach,
  Here it comes!

"Lasagna"   *—X. J. Kennedy*

First lines: "Wouldn't you love / To have lasagna"

This poem can be found in the following:
  Hopkins, Lee Bennett. *April, Bubbles, Chocolate: An ABC of Poetry.* Illus. by
    Barry Root. New York: Simon and Schuster Books for Young Readers,
    1994.
  Janeczko, Paul B. *Pocket Poems Selected for a Journey.* New York: Bradbury,
    1985.

"Celery"   *—Ogden Nash*

First lines: "Celery, raw / Develops the jaw"

This poem can be found in the following:
  Brett, Simon. *The Faber Book of Useful Verse.* London: Faber and Faber,
    1981.

Ferris, Helen Josephine. *Favorite Poems: Old and New.* Illus. by Leonard Weisgard. Garden City, NY: Doubleday, 1957.

Prelutsky, Jack, ed. *The Random House Book of Poetry for Children.* Illus. by Arnold Lobel. New York: Random House, 1983.

"Ketchup" —*Anon.*

When you tip a ketchup bottle,
First will come a little, then a lot'll.

"Peas" —*Anon.*

I eat my peas with honey;
I've done it all my life.
It makes the peas taste funny,
But it keeps them on my knife.

"Oodles of Noodles" —*Lucia M. Hymes and James L. Hymes Jr.*

First line: "I love noodles. Give me oodles."

This poem can be found in the following:
Prelutsky, Jack, ed. *The Random House Book of Poetry for Children.* Illus. by Arnold Lobel. New York: Random House, 1983.

"Yellow Butter" —*Mary Ann Hoberman*

First line: "Yellow butter purple jelly red jam black bread"

This poem can be found in the following:
Prelutsky, Jack, ed. *Read-Aloud Rhymes for the Very Young.* Illus. by Marc Brown. New York: Knopf, 1986.
Rosen, Michael, ed. *The Kingfisher Book of Children's Poetry.* New York: Kingfisher, 1993.

"Arbuckle Jones" —*Peter Wesley-Smith*

First lines: "Arbuckle Jones / When flustered"

This poem can be found in the following:
Janeczko, Paul B. *This Delicious Day: 65 Poems.* New York: Orchard, 1987.

"Lemonade"   *—Pyke Johnson Jr.*

First line: "Lemons are yellow"

This poem can be found in the following:
> Cole, William. *Poem Stew.* Illus. by Karen Ann Weinhaus. New York: Lippincott, 1981.

"I Should Have Stayed in Bed Today"   *—Jack Prelutsky*

First lines: "I should have stayed in bed today, / In bed's where I belong"

This poem can be found in the following:
> Rising Writer, at http://risingwriterblog.blogspot.com/2006/10/i-should -have-stayed-in-bed-today-by.html.

"My Little Sister"   *—William Wise*

First lines: "My little sister / likes to eat"

This poem can be found in the following:
> Prelutsky, Jack, ed. *The Random House Book of Poetry for Children.* Illus. by Arnold Lobel. New York: Random House, 1983.

"My Father Owns the Butcher Shop"   *—Anon.*

> My father owns the butcher shop,
> My mother cuts the meat
> And I'm the little hot dog
> That runs around the street.

"Sneaky Bill"   *—William Cole*

First line: "I'm Sneaky Bill, I'm terrible and mean and vicious"

This poem can be found in the following:
> Cole, William. *Poem Stew.* Illus. by Karen Ann Weinhaus. New York: Lippincott, 1981.

"My Mouth"   *—Arnold Adoff*

First lines: "stay shut / but / food just / finds / a way"

This poem can be found in the following:
> Prelutsky, Jack, ed. *The Random House Book of Poetry for Children.* Illus. by Arnold Lobel. New York: Random House, 1983.

"Accidentally"   —*Maxine W. Kumin*

First line: "Once—I didn't mean to, but that was that—"

This poem can be found in the following:
> Prelutsky, Jack, ed. *The Random House Book of Poetry for Children.* Illus. by Arnold Lobel. New York: Random House, 1983.

"Eat-It-All-Elaine"   —*Kaye Starbird*

First lines: "I went away last August / To summer camp in Maine"

This poem can be found in the following:
> Larrick, Nancy. *Piping down the Valleys Wild: Poetry for the Young of All Ages.* Illus. by Ellen Raskin. New York: Bantam Doubleday Dell Books for Young Readers, 1999.
> Prelutsky, Jack, ed. *The Random House Book of Poetry for Children.* Illus. by Arnold Lobel. New York: Random House, 1983.

"A Thousand Hairy Savages"   —*Spike Milligan*

First lines: "A thousand hairy savages / Sitting down to lunch."

This poem can be found in the following:
> Baker, Russell, ed. *The Norton Book of Light Verse.* New York: Norton, 1986.
> Cole, William. *Pith and Vinegar: An Anthology of Short Humorous Poetry.* New York: Simon and Schuster, 1969.
> Corrin, Sara, and Stephen Corrin. *Once Upon a Rhyme: 101 Poems for Young Children.* Illus. by Jill Bennett. London: Faber and Faber, 1982.
> Prelutsky, Jack, ed. *The Random House Book of Poetry for Children.* Illus. by Arnold Lobel. New York: Random House, 1983.

"A Peanut Sat on a Railroad Track"   —*Anon.*

A peanut sat on a railroad track,
His heart was all a-flutter;
The five-fifteen came rushing by—
Toot! Toot! Peanut butter!

"The Pizza" *—Ogden Nash*

First line: "Look at itsy-bitsy Mitzi!"

This poem can be found in the following (as part of a larger work, Table Talk*):*
Nash, Ogden. *Verses from 1929 On.* Boston: Little, Brown, 1959.

"Toaster" *—William Jay Smith*

First line: "A silver scaled dragon with jaws flaming red"

This poem can be found in the following:
Austin, Mary C., and Queenie Beatrice Mills. *The Sound of Poetry.* Boston: Allyn and Bacon, 1963.
Harrison, Michael, ed. *The Oxford Treasury of Children's Poems.* Oxford University Press, 1995.
Prelutsky, Jack, ed. *The Random House Book of Poetry for Children.* Illus. by Arnold Lobel. New York: Random House, 1983.
Prelutsky, Jack, ed. *Read-Aloud Rhymes for the Very Young.* Illus. by Marc Brown. New York: Knopf, 1986.
Smith, William Jay. *A Green Place: Modern Poems.* Illus. by Jacques Hnizdovsky. New York: Delacorte/Seymour Lawrence, 1982.

"Song of the Pop-Bottlers" *—Morris Bishop*

First lines: "Pop bottles pop-bottles / in pop shops"

This poem can be found in the following:
Cole, William, ed. *The Fireside Book of Humorous Poetry.* New York: Simon and Schuster, 1959.
Ferris, Helen Josephine. *Favorite Poems: Old and New.* Illus. by Leonard Weisgard. Garden City, NY: Doubleday, 1957.
Kennedy, X. J., and Dorothy M. Kennedy. *Knock at a Star: A Child's Introduction to Poetry.* Illus. by Karen Ann Weinhaus. Boston: Little, Brown, 1982.

"It's Such a Shock, I Almost Screech" *—William Cole*

First lines: "It's such a shock, I almost screech, / When I find a worm inside my peach!"

This poem can be found in the following:
Cole, William. *Poem Stew.* Illus. by Karen Ann Weinhaus. New York: Lippincott, 1981.

Prelutsky, Jack, ed. *Read-Aloud Rhymes for the Very Young.* Illus. by Marc Brown. New York: Knopf, 1986.

"Mary Had a Little Lamb" —*Anon.*

Mary had a little lamb,
You've heard this tale before;
But did you know
She passed her plate
And had a little more?

"Bubble Gum" —*Nina Payne*

First line: "I'm in trouble"

This poem can be found in the following:
Prelutsky, Jack, ed. *The Random House Book of Poetry for Children.* Illus. by Arnold Lobel. New York: Random House, 1983.

"Table Manners" —*Gelett Burgess*

The Goops they lick their fingers,
—And the Goops they lick their knives;
They spill their broth on the tablecloth;
—Oh, they live untidy lives.

The Goops they talk while eating,
—And loud and fast they chew,
So that is why I am glad that I
—Am not a Goop. Are you?

This poem can be found in the following:
Hall, Donald, ed. *The Oxford Book of Children's Verse in America.* New York: Oxford University Press, 1985.
Prelutsky, Jack, ed. *The Random House Book of Poetry for Children.* Illus. by Arnold Lobel. New York: Random House, 1983.
Prelutsky, Jack, ed. *Read-Aloud Rhymes for the Very Young.* Illus. by Marc Brown. New York: Knopf, 1986.

"Here Lies a Greedy Girl" —*Anon.*

Here lies a greedy girl, Jane Bevan,
Whose breakfasts hardly ever stopped.

One morning at half past eleven
She snapped, then crackled, then popped.

"This Is Just to Say" *—William Carlos Williams*

First lines: "I have eaten / the plums / that were in / the icebox"

This poem can be found in the following:

Ciardi, John. *How Does a Poem Mean?* Boston: Houghton Mifflin, 1960.

Kennedy, X. J., and Dorothy M. Kennedy. *Knock at a Star: A Child's Introduction to Poetry.* Illus. by Karen Ann Weinhaus. Boston: Little, Brown, 1982.

Prelutsky, Jack, ed. *The Random House Book of Poetry for Children.* Illus. by Arnold Lobel. New York: Random House, 1983.

"Egg Thoughts" *—Russell Hoban*

First line: "I do not like the way you slide"

This poem can be found in the following:

Cole, Joanna. *A New Treasury of Children's Poetry: Old Favorites and New Discoveries.* Illus. by Judith Gwyn Brown. Garden City, NY: Doubleday, 1984.

Harrison, Michael, ed. *The Oxford Treasury of Children's Poems.* Oxford University Press, 1995.

Prelutsky, Jack, ed. *The Random House Book of Poetry for Children.* Illus. by Arnold Lobel. New York: Random House, 1983.

"Mummy Slept Late and Daddy Fixed Breakfast" *—John Ciardi*

First line: "Daddy fixed breakfast"

This poem can be found in the following:

Larrick, Nancy. *Piping down the Valleys Wild: Poetry for the Young of All Ages.* Illus. by Ellen Raskin. New York: Bantam Doubleday Dell Books for Young Readers, 1999.

Prelutsky, Jack, ed. *The Random House Book of Poetry for Children.* Illus. by Arnold Lobel. New York: Random House, 1983.

Topic: Limericks

There was an Old Man with a beard,
Who said, "It is just as I feared!—
Two Owls and a Hen, four Larks and a Wren,
Have all built their nests in my beard."

—*Edward Lear*

There was a young hopeful named Sam
Who loved diving into the jam.
When his mother said, "Sammy!
Don't make yourself jammy."
He said, "You're too late Ma, I am."

—*Elizabeth Ripley*

There was an old man of Blackheath,
Who sat on his set of false teeth.
Said he, with a start,
"Oh, Lord bless my heart!'
I've bitten myself underneath!"

—*Anon.*

A tutor who tooted a flute
Tried to teach two young tutors to toot.
—Said the two to the tutor,
—"Is it harder to toot, or
To tutor two tutors to toot?"

—*Carolyn Wells*

I raised a great hullaballoo
When I found a large mouse in my stew.
Said the waiter, "Don't shout
Or wave it about
Or the rest will be wanting one too!"

—*Anon.*

There was a young lady of Ryde
Who ate a green apple and died.
The apple fermented
Within the lamented
And made cider inside her inside.

—*Anon.*

There was a young lady of Niger
Who smiled as she rode on a tiger;
They returned from the ride
With the lady inside,
And a smile on the face of the tiger.

—*Anon.*

There was an old man from Peru
Who dreamed he was eating his shoe;
He woke in a fright
In the middle of the night
And found it was perfectly true.

—Anon.

Topic: Nature and Seasons

"Weather"
—Anon.

Whether the weather be fine
Or whether the weather be not,
Whether the weather be cold
Or whether the weather be hot,
We'll weather the weather,
Whether we like it or not.

"Now"
—Prince Redcloud

First lines: "Close the barbecue / Close the sun"

This poem can be found in the following:
Hopkins, Lee Bennett. *The Sky Is Full of Song.* Illus. by Dirk Zimmer. New York: Harper and Row, 1983.

"New Sounds to Walk on Today"
—Lilian Moore

New sounds to
Walk on
Today
Dry leaves,
Talking
In hoarse
Whispers,
Under bare trees.

"Hungry Morning"   —*Myra Cohn Livingston*

First line: "In December I remember in the rain and frosty snow"

This poem can be found in the following:
> Hopkins, Lee Bennett. *The Sky Is Full of Song.* Illus. by Dirk Zimmer. New York: Harper and Row, 1983.

"Fair Warning"   —*Norah Smaridge*

First line: "If you go out without your coat"

This poem can be found in the following:
> Hopkins, Lee Bennett. *I Think I Saw a Snail; Young Poems for City Seasons.* Illus. by Harold Laymont James. New York: Crown, 1969.

"March and I Are Different"   —*Third Grade Student, Westing School, Virginia*

> March comes in like a lion
> March goes out like a lamb
> But I go in and out of March
> Just as I am.

"Who Has Seen the Wind?"   —*Christina Rossetti*

> Who has seen the wind?
> Neither I nor you:
> But when the leaves hang trembling,
> The wind is passing through.
>
> Who has seen the wind?
> Neither you nor I:
> But when the trees bow down their heads,
> The wind is passing by.

"Spring"   —*William Blake*

> Sound the flute!
> Now't is mute;
> Birds delight,
> Day and night,

In the dale,
Lark in sky,
Merrily,
Merrily, merrily to welcome in the year.

"Leaves" —*Paul Walker*

First lines: "The leaves fall / like big pennies"

This poem can be found in the following:
Larrick, Nancy. *Piping down the Valleys Wild: Poetry for the Young of All Ages.* Illus. by Ellen Raskin. New York: Bantam Doubleday Dell Books for Young Readers, 1999.

"You Cannot Hide in Snow" —*Anon.*

You cannot hide in snow
No matter where you go
You always leave a trail behind
That others always find.

"Winter Moon" —*Langston Hughes*

First line: "How thin and sharp is the moon tonight!"

This poem can be found in the following:
Hughes, Langston. *The Collected Poems of Langston Hughes.* New York: Knopf, 1994.

"Stopping by Woods on a Snowy Evening" —*Robert Frost*

First line: "Whose woods these are I think I know"

This poem can be found in the following:
Arbuthnot, May Hill, and Shelton L. Root, eds. *Time for Poetry: A Representative Collection of Poetry for Children, to Be Used in the Classroom, Home, or Camp; Especially Planned for College Classes in Children's Literature.* Illus. by Arthur Paul. Glenview, IL: Scott, Foresman, 1967.
Ciardi, John. *How Does a Poem Mean?* Boston: Houghton Mifflin, 1960.
Cole, Joanna. *A New Treasury of Children's Poetry: Old Favorites and New Discoveries.* Illus. by Judith Gwyn Brown. Garden City, NY: Doubleday, 1984.

de Regniers, Beatrice Schenk, ed. *Sing a Song of Popcorn: Every Child's Book of Poems.* Illus. by Marcia Brown. New York: Scholastic, 1988.

Larrick, Nancy. *Piping down the Valleys Wild: Poetry for the Young of All Ages.* Illus. by Ellen Raskin. New York: Bantam Doubleday Dell Books for Young Readers, 1999.

Prelutsky, Jack, ed. *Read-Aloud Rhymes for the Very Young.* Illus. by Marc Brown. New York: Knopf, 1986.

Smith, William Jay. *A Green Place: Modern Poems.* Illus. by Jacques Hnizdovsky. New York: Delacorte/Seymour Lawrence, 1982.

Sword, Elizabeth Hauge, and Victoria McCarthy, eds. *A Child's Anthology of Poetry.* Illus. by Tom Pohrt. Hopewell, NJ: Ecco, 1995.

"Spring"   —*Karla Kuskin*

First lines: "I'm shouting / I'm singing"

This poem can be found in the following:

Larrick, Nancy. *Piping down the Valleys Wild: Poetry for the Young of All Ages.* Illus. by Ellen Raskin. New York: Delacorte, 1968.

Prelutsky, Jack, ed. *The Random House Book of Poetry for Children.* Illus. by Arnold Lobel. New York: Random House, 1983.

"Spring Rain"   —*Marchette Chute*

First line: "The storm came up so very quick"

This poem can be found in the following:

Arbuthnot, May Hill, and Shelton L. Root, eds. *Time for Poetry: A Representative Collection of Poetry for Children, to Be Used in the Classroom, Home, or Camp; Especially Planned for College Classes in Children's Literature.* Illus. by Arthur Paul. Glenview, IL: Scott, Foresman, 1967.

Prelutsky, Jack, ed. *The Random House Book of Poetry for Children.* Illus. by Arnold Lobel. New York: Random House, 1983.

"June"   —*Myra Cohn Livingston*

First lines: "The sun is rich, / and gladly pays"

This poem can be found in the following:

Updike, John. *A Child's Calendar.* Illus. by Trina Schart Hyman. New York: Holiday House, 1999.

"November Night" —*Adelaide Crapsey*

First lines: Listen . . . / With faint dry sound,

This poem can be found in the following:
>   Ferris, Helen Josephine. *Favorite Poems: Old and New.* Illus. by Leonard
>   Weisgard. Garden City, NY: Doubleday, 1957.
>   Poetry Foundation, at www.poetryfoundation.org/poem/175524.

"Over the Wintry Forest" —*Soseki (Haiku)*

>   Over the wintry
>   Forest, winds howl in a rage
>   With no leaves to blow.

"I Heard a Bird Sing" —*Oliver Herford*

First lines: "I heard a bird sing / In the dark of December"

This poem can be found in the following:
>   Cole, Joanna. *A New Treasury of Children's Poetry: Old Favorites and New
>   Discoveries.* Illus. by Judith Gwyn Brown. Garden City, NY: Doubleday,
>   1984.
>   de Regniers, Beatrice Schenk, ed. *Sing a Song of Popcorn: Every Child's Book
>   of Poems.* Illus. by Marcia Brown. New York: Scholastic, 1988.
>   Larrick, Nancy. P*iping down the Valleys Wild: Poetry for the Young of All
>   Ages.* Illus. by Ellen Raskin. New York: Bantam Doubleday Dell Books
>   for Young Readers, 1999.
>   Prelutsky, Jack, ed. *The Random House Book of Poetry for Children.* Illus. by
>   Arnold Lobel. New York: Random House, 1983.

"When" —*Dorothy Aldiss*

First lines: "In February there are days / Blue, and nearly warm"

This poem can be found in the following:
>   Lower School Poetry Archive RSS, at http://blog.lrei.org/ls-poetry-archive/
>   brooms-dorothy-aldis.

"Swift Things Are Beautiful" —*Elizabeth Coatsworth*

First line: "Swift things are beautiful."

This poem can be found in the following:
> Sword, Elizabeth Hauge, and Victoria McCarthy, eds. *A Child's Anthology of Poetry.* Illus. by Tom Pohrt. Hopewell, NJ: Ecco, 1995.

"City Rain" —*Rachel Field*

First line: "Rain in the city!"

This poem can be found in the following:
> Arbuthnot, May Hill, and Shelton L. Root, eds. *Time for Poetry: A Representative Collection of Poetry for Children, to Be Used in the Classroom, Home, or Camp; Especially Planned for College Classes in Children's Literature.* Illus. by Arthur Paul. Glenview, IL: Scott, Foresman, 1967.
> Austin, Mary C., and Queenie Beatrice Mills. *The Sound of Poetry.* Boston: Allyn and Bacon, 1963.

"Snow toward Evening" —*Melville Cane*

First line: "Suddenly the sky turned grey"

This poem can be found in the following:
> Arbuthnot, May Hill, and Shelton L. Root, eds. *Time for Poetry: A Representative Collection of Poetry for Children, to Be Used in the Classroom, Home, or Camp; Especially Planned for College Classes in Children's Literature.* Illus. by Arthur Paul. Glenview, IL: Scott, Foresman, 1967.
> Larrick, Nancy. P*iping down the Valleys Wild: Poetry for the Young of All Ages.* Illus. by Ellen Raskin. New York: Bantam Doubleday Dell Books for Young Readers, 1999.

Song of Solomon 2:11–12

> For Lo, the Winter is past,
> The rain is over and gone;
> The flowers appear on the Earth;
> The time of the singing of birds is come,
> And the voice of the turtle is heard in our land.

"Pippa's Song" (Variant title "Spring Song") —*Robert Browning*

> The year's at the spring,
> And day's at the morn;
> Morning's at seven;

The hillside's dew-pearled;
The lark's on the wing;
The snail's on the thorn:
God's in His Heaven—
All's right with the world!

Topic: People and Things

"Bubbles"   —*Carl Sandburg*

First line: "Two bubbles found they had rainbows on their curves"

This poem can be found in the following:
Janeczko, Paul B. *This Delicious Day: 65 Poems.* New York: Orchard, 1987.
Sandburg, Carl. *The Complete Poems of Carl Sandburg.* New York: Harcourt
    Brace Jovanovich, 1970.

"Foolish Questions"   —*American folk rhyme adapted by William Cole*

First line: "Where can a man buy a cap for his knee?"

This poem can be found in the following:
Lansky, Bruce. *Kids Pick the Funniest Poems.* Illus. by Stephen Carpenter.
    Deephaven, MN: Meadowbrook, 1991.

"My Favorite Word"   —*Lucia M. Hymes and James L. Hymes Jr.*

There is one word, my favorite
The very, very best
It isn't "no" or "maybe"
It's yes, yes, yes, yes, yes.

"Yes you may," and "Yes, of course,"
And "Yes, please help yourself,"
And when I want a piece of cake,
"Why yes, it's on the shelf,"

Some candy, "Yes."
A cookie, "Yes."
A movie, "Yes, we'll go."
I love it when they say my word:
"Yes, yes, yes," not "No."

"Going to Bed"   —*Marchette Chute*

I'm always told to hurry up-
Which I'd be glad to do,
If there were not so many things
That need attending to.

But first I have to find my towel
Which fell behind the rack,
And when a pillow's thrown at me
I have to throw it back.

And then I have to get the things
I need in bed with me.
Like marbles and my birthday train
And Pete the chimpanzee.

I have to see my polliwog
Is safely in its pan,
And stand a minute on my head
To be quite sure I can.

I have to bounce upon my bed
To see if it will sink,
And then when I am covered up
I find I need a drink. —Marchette Chute

This poem can be found in the following:
Sleeping and Waking, at www.dennydavis.net/poemfiles/sleep.htm

---

"On the Ning Nang Nong"   —*Spike Milligan*

First lines: "On the ning nang nong / Where the cows go bong"

This poem can be found in the following:
Prelutsky, Jack, ed. *The Random House Book of Poetry for Children.* Illus. by
Arnold Lobel. New York: Random House, 1983.

"Band-Aids"   —*Shel Silverstein*

First line: "I have a Band-Aid on my finger"

This poem can be found in the following:
Silverstein, Shel, author and illus. *Where the Sidewalk Ends: The Poems &*
Drawings of Shel Silverstein. New York: Harper and Row, 1974.

(When sharing this poem you can make a cartoon man and place Band-Aids on him as the poem is read—or just have someone count the Band-Aids.)

"The Folk Who Live in Backward Town"   —*Mary Ann Hoberman*

First lines: "The folk who live in backward town / are inside out and upside down"

This poem can be found in the following:
>   de Regniers, Beatrice Schenk, ed. *Sing a Song of Popcorn: Every Child's Book of Poems.* Illus. by Marcia Brown. New York: Scholastic, 1988.
>   Hall, Donald, ed. *The Oxford Book of Children's Verse in America.* New York: Oxford University Press, 1985.
>   Hall, Donald, ed. *The Oxford Illustrated Book of American Children's Poems.* New York: Oxford University Press, 1999.
>   Prelutsky, Jack, ed. *The Random House Book of Poetry for Children.* Illus. by Arnold Lobel. New York: Random House, 1983.

"Adventures of Isabel"   —*Ogden Nash*

First line: "Isabel, Isabel, didn't care"

This poem can be found in the following:
>   Prelutsky, Jack, ed. *The Random House Book of Poetry for Children.* Illus. by Arnold Lobel. New York: Random House, 1983.

"Tuesday I Was Ten, and Though"   —*Kaye Starbird*

First lines: "Tuesday I was ten, and though / the fact delights me plenty"

This poem can be found in the following:
>   Starbird, Kaye. *Don't Ever Cross a Crocodile, and Other Poems.* Philadelphia: Lippincott, 1963.

"Just Me"   —*Margaret Hillert*

First line: "Nobody sees what I can see"

This poem can be found in the following:
>   Prelutsky, Jack, ed. *The Random House Book of Poetry for Children.* Illus. by Arnold Lobel. New York: Random House, 1983.

"When I Was Lost"   —*Dorothy Aldis*

First lines: "Underneath my belt / My stomach was a stone"

This poem can be found in the following:
Prelutsky, Jack, ed. *The Random House Book of Poetry for Children.* Illus. by
Arnold Lobel. New York: Random House, 1983.

"My Nose"   —*Dorothy Aldis*

First lines: "It doesn't breath / It doesn't smell"

This poem can be found in the following:
Prelutsky, Jack, ed. *The Random House Book of Poetry for Children.* Illus. by
Arnold Lobel. New York: Random House, 1983.

"I Think"   —*Danny Schwartz and Mike McMahan*

I think
My dog chewed it,
My sister glued it,
My mother cooked it,
My brother hooked it,
My Dad mailed it to Naperville
So I'm looking for my paper still.

Examples of cinquain:

Pet
Soft Brown
Jumps, runs, sleeps
My best loved pal
Kitten

Flopsy
Soft Cuddly
Arms flopping Hanging
I love her so
Doll

Colt
All legs
Wobbling, shaking, kicking
Curious, full of life
Pony

"Sing a Song of Subways" —*Eve Merriam*

First lines: "Sing a song of subways / Never see the sun"

This poem can be found in the following:
    Kennedy, X. J., and Dorothy M. Kennedy. *Knock at a Star: A Child's Intro-duction to Poetry.* Illus. by Karen Ann Weinhaus. Boston: Little, Brown, 1982.
    Prelutsky, Jack, ed. *The Random House Book of Poetry for Children.* Illus. by Arnold Lobel. New York: Random House, 1983.

"Far Trek" —*June Brady*

First line: "Some things will never change although"

This poem can be found in the following:
    Brewton, Sara Westbrook, John Edmund Brewton, and John Brewton Blackburn, contributors. *Of Quarks, Quasars, and Other Quirks: Quiz-zical Poems for the Supersonic Age.* Illus. by Quentin Blake. New York: Crowell, 1977.
    Prelutsky, Jack, ed. *The Random House Book of Poetry for Children.* Illus. by Arnold Lobel. New York: Random House, 1983.

"Sing a Song of People" —*Lois Lenski*

First lines: "Sing a song of people / walking fast or slow"

This poem can be found in the following:
    Harrison, Michael, ed. *The Oxford Treasury of Children's Poems.* Oxford: Oxford University Press, 1995.
    Philip, Neil, ed. *The New Oxford Book of Children's Verse.* Oxford: Oxford University Press, 1996.
    Prelutsky, Jack, ed. *The Random House Book of Poetry for Children.* Illus. by Arnold Lobel. New York: Random House, 1983.

"Thoughts on Talkers" —*Walter Brooks*

First line: "Some people talk in a telephone"

This poem can be found in the following:
> Prelutsky, Jack, ed. *The Random House Book of Poetry for Children.* Illus. by Arnold Lobel. New York: Random House, 1983.

"People" —*Charlotte Zolotow*

First lines: "Some people talk and talk / and never say a thing"

This poem can be found in the following:
> Prelutsky, Jack, ed. *The Random House Book of Poetry for Children.* Illus. by Arnold Lobel. New York: Random House, 1983.

"Miss T." —*Walter De La Mare*

It's a very odd thing—
  odd as can be—
That whatever Miss T. eats
  turns into Miss T.;

Porridge and apples,
  mince, muffins and mutton,
Jam, junket, jumbles—
  not a rap, nor a button

It matters; the moment
  They're out of her plate,
Though shared by Miss Butcher
  and sour Mr. Bate;

Tiny and cheerful,
  and neat as can be,
Whatever Miss T. eats
  turns into Miss T.

This poem can be found in the following:
> Larrick, Nancy. *Piping down the Valleys Wild: Poetry for the Young of All Ages.* Illus. by Ellen Raskin. New York: Bantam Doubleday Dell Books for Young Readers, 1999.

"Daddy Fell into the Pond" —*Alfred Noyes*

Everyone grumbled. The sky was grey.
We had nothing to do and nothing to say.
We were nearing the end of a dismal day,
And there seemed to be nothing beyond,

THEN
Daddy fell into the pond!

And everyone's face grew merry and bright,
And Timothy danced for sheer delight.
"Give me the camera, quick, oh quick!
He's crawling out of the duckweed." Click!

Then the gardener suddenly slapped his knee,
And doubled up, shaking silently,
And the ducks all quacked as if they were daft
And it sounded as if the old drake laughed.

O, there wasn't a thing that didn't respond
WHEN
Daddy fell into the pond!

This poem can be found in the following:

Ferris, Helen Josephine. *Favorite Poems: Old and New.* Illus. by Leonard
    Weisgard. Garden City, NY: Doubleday, 1957.
Larrick, Nancy. *Piping down the Valleys Wild: Poetry for the Young of All
    Ages.* Illus. by Ellen Raskin. New York: Delacorte, 1968.
Philip, Neil, ed. *The New Oxford Book of Children's Verse.* Oxford: Oxford
    University Press, 1996.
Prelutsky, Jack, ed. *The Random House Book of Poetry for Children.* Illus. by
    Arnold Lobel. New York: Random House, 1983.
Sword, Elizabeth Hauge, and Victoria McCarthy, eds. *A Child's Anthology of
    Poetry.* Illus. by Tom Pohrt. Hopewell, NJ: Ecco, 1995.

"Hello, Is This Number One-One-One-One?" —*William Cole*

"Hello, is this number one-one-one-one?"
"No, this is eleven-eleven."
"Oh, sorry to have bothered you."
"That's okay, I had to get up anyway to answer the phone."

"George Washington Is Tops with Me" —*Shel Silverstein*

First lines: "George Washington is tops with me / for he cut down the cherry tree"

This poem can be found in the following:

Cole, William. *Poems for Seasons and Celebrations.* Illus. by Johannes
    Troyer. Cleveland: World, 1961.

"The Base Stealer"   —*Robert Francis*

First line: "Poised between going on and back, pulled"

This poem can be found in the following:

Cole, Joanna. *A New Treasury of Children's Poetry: Old Favorites and New Discoveries.* Illus. by Judith Gwyn Brown. Garden City, NY: Doubleday, 1984.

Prelutsky, Jack, ed. *The Random House Book of Poetry for Children.* Illus. by Arnold Lobel. New York: Random House, 1983.

"Buffalo Dusk"   —*Carl Sandburg*

The buffaloes are gone.
And those who saw the buffaloes are gone.
Those who saw the buffaloes by thousands and how they pawed the prairie sod into dust with their hoofs, their great heads down pawing on in a great pageant of dusk,
Those who saw the buffaloes are gone.
And the buffaloes are gone.

This poem can be found in the following:

Arbuthnot, May Hill, and Shelton L. Root, eds. *Time for Poetry: A Representative Collection of Poetry for Children, to Be Used in the Classroom, Home, or Camp; Especially Planned for College Classes in Children's Literature.* Illus. by Arthur Paul. Glenview, IL: Scott, Foresman, 1967.

de Regniers, Beatrice Schenk, ed. *Sing a Song of Popcorn: Every Child's Book of Poems.* Illus. by Marcia Brown. New York: Scholastic, 1988.

Hall, Donald, ed. *The Oxford Book of Children's Verse in America.* New York: Oxford University Press, 1985.

Larrick, Nancy. *Piping down the Valleys Wild: Poetry for the Young of All Ages.* Illus. by Ellen Raskin. New York: Bantam Doubleday Dell Books for Young Readers, 1999.

Prelutsky, Jack, ed. *The Random House Book of Poetry for Children.* Illus. by Arnold Lobel. New York: Random House, 1983.

Sandburg, Carl. *The Complete Poems of Carl Sandburg.* New York: Harcourt Brace Jovanovich, 1970.

Sword, Elizabeth Hauge, and Victoria McCarthy, eds. *A Child's Anthology of Poetry.* Illus. by Tom Pohrt. Hopewell, NJ: Ecco, 1995.

"I, Too" —*Langston Hughes*

First line: "I, too, sing America."

This poem can be found in the following:
> Hughes, Langston. *The Collected Poems of Langston Hughes.* New York:
> Knopf, 1994.

"The Little Boy and the Old Man" —*Shel Silverstein*

First line: "Said the little boy, 'Sometimes I drop my spoon'"

This poem can be found in the following:
> Silverstein, Shel, author and illus. *A Light in the Attic.* New York: Harper
> and Row, 1981.
> Prelutsky, Jack, ed. *The Random House Book of Poetry for Children.* Illus. by
> Arnold Lobel. New York: Random House, 1983.

"Get Up and Bar the Door" —*Anon.*

It fell about the Martinmas time,
And a gay time it was then,
When our good wife got puddings to make,
And she's boiled them in the pan.

The wind so cold blew south and north,
And blew into the floor;
Quoth our goodman to our goodwife,
"Gat out and bar the door."

"My hand is in my household work
Goodman, as ye may see;
An it should not be barred for a hundred years,
It's no be barred for me."

They made a pact between them both,
They made it firm and sure,
That whosoe'er should speak the first,
Should rise and bar the door.

Then by there came two gentlemen,
At twelve o'clock at night,
And they could neither see house nor hall,
Nor coal nor candlelight.

"Now whether is this a rich man's house,
Or whether is it a poor?"
But never a word would one of them speak,
For barring of the door.

The guests they ate the white puddings,
And then they ate the black;
Tho much the goodwife thought to herself,
Yet never a word she spake.

Then said the one stranger to the other,
"Here, man, take ye my knife;
Do ye take off the old man's beard,
And I'll kiss the goodwife."

"But there's no hot water to scrape it off,
And what shall we do than?"
"Then why not use the pudding broth,
That boils into the pan?"

O up then started our goodman,
An angry man was he:
"Will ye kiss my wife before my eyes
And with pudding broth scald me?"

Then up and started our goodwife,
Gave three skips on the floor:
"Goodman, you've spoken the very first word,
Get up and bar the door!"

This poem can be found in the following:
Larrick, Nancy. *Piping down the Valleys Wild: Poetry for the Young of All Ages.* Illus. by Ellen Raskin. New York: Bantam Doubleday Dell Books for Young Readers, 1999.

"Some Things Don't Make Any Sense at All" —*Judith Viorst*

First line: "My mom says I'm her sugarplum"

This poem can be found in the following:
Poemhunter.com, at www.poemhunter.com/poem/some-things-don-t -make-any-sense-at-all.
Prelutsky, Jack, ed. *The Random House Book of Poetry for Children.* Illus. by Arnold Lobel. New York: Random House, 1983.

"Remember Me?" —*Judith Viorst*

First lines: "What will they say / When I've gone away?"

This poem can be found in the following:
Poems for Children & Big Kids Too! Fun & Silly from Brownielocks, at
www.brownielocks.com/childrenspoems.html.

"Ode to a Sneeze" —*attributed to G. Wallace*

First line: "I sneezed a sneeze into the air"

This poem can be found in the following:
Prelutsky, Jack. *For Laughing Out Loud: Poems to Tickle Your Funnybone.*
Illus. by Marjorie Priceman. New York: Knopf, 1991.

"Catherine" —*Karla Kuskin*

First line: "Catherine said, 'I think I'll bake/a most delicious chocolate cake'"

This poem can be found in the following:
Cole, Joanna. *A New Treasury of Children's Poetry: Old Favorites and New Dis-
coveries.* Illus. by Judith Gwyn Brown. Garden City, NY: Doubleday, 1984.
Larrick, Nancy. *Piping down the Valleys Wild: Poetry for the Young of All
Ages.* Illus. by Ellen Raskin. New York: Bantam Doubleday Dell Books
for Young Readers, 1999.

"What Someone Said When He Was Spanked —*John Ciardi*
on the Day before His Birthday"

First lines: "Some day / I may / Pack my bag and run away"

This poem can be found in the following:
Prelutsky, Jack, ed. *The Random House Book of Poetry for Children.* Illus. by
Arnold Lobel. New York: Random House, 1983.

"Stanley the Fierce" —*Judith Viorst*

First lines: "Stanley the fierce / Has a chipped front tooth"

This poem can be found in the following:
Viorst, Judith. *If I Were in Charge of the World: And Other Worries.* New
York: Aladdin, 1981.

"Sneakers, Sneakers" —*Julio Mora and Adam Brenner*

Sneakers, sneakers
Everywhere
Whenever I stare
They are there
On courts
In sports
In different colors
And sorts.

"Misnomer" —*Eve Merriam*

First lines: "If you've ever been one / You know that"

This poem can be found in the following:
Prelutsky, Jack, ed. *The Random House Book of Poetry for Children.* Illus. by Arnold Lobel. New York: Random House, 1983.

"Mr. Mulligan's Window" —*Jack Prelutsky*

First line: "We broke Mr. Mulligan's window"

This poem can be found in the following:
Prelutsky, Jack. *Rolling Harvey down the Hill.* Illus. by Victoria Chess. New York: Greenwillow, 1980.

"Nightmare" —*Judith Viorst*

First lines: "Beautiful, beautiful Beverly / has asked me to the dance"

This poem can be found in the following:
Poetry, at www.angelfire.com/ms2/leighbertonline/poetry.htm#Nightmare.

"Insomnia the Gem of the Ocean" —*John Updike*

First line: "When I lay me down to sleep"

This poem can be found in the following:
Baker, Russell, ed. *The Norton Book of Light Verse.* New York: Norton, 1986.
Brewton, Sara Westbrook, John Edmund Brewton, and John Brewton Blackburn, contributors. *Of Quarks, Quasars, and Other Quirks: Quizzical Poems for the Supersonic Age.* Illus. by Quentin Blake. New York: Crowell, 1977.

Janeczko, Paul B. *Don't Forget to Fly: A Cycle of Modern Poems.* Scarsdale, NY: Bradbury, 1981.

"Hot Line" —*Louella Dunann*

First lines: "Our daughter, Alicia / has just turned sixteen"

This poem can be found in the following:

Brewton, Sara Westbrook, John Edmund Brewton, and John Brewton Blackburn, contributors. *Of Quarks, Quasars, and Other Quirks: Quizzical Poems for the Supersonic Age.* Illus. by Quentin Blake. New York: Crowell, 1977.

Prelutsky, Jack, ed. *The Random House Book of Poetry for Children.* Illus. by Arnold Lobel. New York: Random House, 1983.

"Arithmetic" —*Carl Sandburg*

Arithmetic is where numbers fly like pigeons in and out of your head.

Arithmetic tells you how many you lose or win if you know how many you had before you lost or won.

Arithmetic is seven eleven all good children go to heaven—or five six bundle of sticks.

Arithmetic is numbers you squeeze from your head to your hand to your pencil to your paper till you get the answer.

Arithmetic is where the answer is right and everything is nice and you can look out the window and see the blue sky—or the answer is wrong and you have to start all over and try again and see how it comes out this time.

This poem can be found in the following:

Sandburg, Carl. *The Complete Poems of Carl Sandburg.* New York: Harcourt Brace Jovanovich, 1970.

"This Is Just to Say" —*William Carlos Williams*

First lines: "This is just to say / I have eaten / the plums / that were in/the icebox"

This poem can be found in the following:

Cole, William, ed. *Pith and Vinegar: An Anthology of Short, Humorous Poetry.* New York: Simon and Schuster, 1969.

Kennedy, X. J., and Dorothy M. Kennedy. *Knock at a Star: A Child's Introduction to Poetry.* Illus. by Karen Ann Weinhaus. Boston: Little, Brown, 1982.

"Variations on a Theme by William Carlos Williams"   —*Kenneth Koch*

First lines: "I chopped down the house that you had been saving
/ to live in next summer"

This poem can be found in the following:
  Poemhunter.com, at www.poemhunter.com/poem/variations-on-a-theme
   -by-william-carlos-williams.

"Mirror rorriM"   —*John Updike*

First line: "When you look Kool Voy Nehw"

This poem can be found in the following:
  Updike, John. *Collected Poems, 1953–1993*. New York: Knopf, 1993.

"A Modern Dragon"   —*Rowena Bastin Bennett*

First line: "A train is a dragon that roars through the dark"

This poem can be found in the following:
  Arbuthnot, May Hill, and Shelton L. Root, eds. *Time for Poetry: A Repre-
   sentative Collection of Poetry for Children, to Be Used in the Classroom,
   Home, or Camp; Especially Planned for College Classes in Children's Litera-
   ture*. Illus. by Arthur Paul. Glenview, IL: Scott, Foresman, 1967.
  Larrick, Nancy. P*iping down the Valleys Wild: Poetry for the Young of All
   Ages*. Illus. by Ellen Raskin. New York: Bantam Doubleday Dell Books
   for Young Readers, 1999.
  Prelutsky, Jack, ed. *Read-Aloud Rhymes for the Very Young*. Illus. by Marc
   Brown. New York: Knopf, 1986.

"The Prayer of the Cat"   —*Carmen Bernos de Gasztold*

First lines: "Lord, / I am the cat"

This poem can be found in the following:
  Larrick, Nancy. *Piping down the Valleys Wild: Poetry for the Young of All
   Ages*. Illus. by Ellen Raskin. New York: Bantam Doubleday Dell Books
   for Young Readers, 1999.

"The Prayer of the Mouse"   —*Carmen Bernos de Gasztold*

First lines: "I am so little and grey, / Dear God"

This poem can be found in the following:
> Larrick, Nancy. *Piping down the Valleys Wild: Poetry for the Young of All Ages.* Illus. by Ellen Raskin. New York: Bantam Doubleday Dell Books for Young Readers, 1999.

"The Prayer of the Old Horse" — *Carmen Bernos de Gasztold*

First lines: "See, Lord, / My coat hangs in tatters"

This poem can be found in the following:
> Larrick, Nancy. *Piping down the Valleys Wild: Poetry for the Young of All Ages.* Illus. by Ellen Raskin. New York: Bantam Doubleday Dell Books for Young Readers, 1999.

"The Prayer of the Goldfish" — *Carmen Bernos de Gasztold*

First line: "Oh, God, Forever I turn in this hard crystal"

This poem can be found in the following:
> Larrick, Nancy. *Piping down the Valleys Wild: Poetry for the Young of All Ages.* Illus. by Ellen Raskin. New York: Bantam Doubleday Dell Books for Young Readers, 1999.

"Apartment House" — *Gerald Rafferty*

First line: "A filing cabinet of human lives"

This poem can be found in the following:
> Brewton, Sara Westbrook, John Edmund Brewton, and Ann Grifalconi. *America Forever New: A Book of Poems.* New York: Crowell, 1968.

"A Sad Song about Greenwich Village" — *Frances Park*

First lines: "She lives in a garret / Up a haunted stair"

This poem can be found in the following:
> Arbuthnot, May Hill, and Shelton L. Root, eds. *Time for Poetry: A Representative Collection of Poetry for Children, to Be Used in the Classroom, Home, or Camp; Especially Planned for College Classes in Children's Literature.* Illus. by Arthur Paul. Glenview, IL: Scott, Foresman, 1967.
> Cole, Joanna. *A New Treasury of Children's Poetry: Old Favorites and New Discoveries.* Illus. by Judith Gwyn Brown. Garden City, NY: Doubleday, 1984.

de Regniers, Beatrice Schenk, ed. *Sing a Song of Popcorn: Every Child's Book of Poems.* Illus. by Marcia Brown. New York: Scholastic, 1988.

Hall, Donald, ed. *The Oxford Book of Children's Verse in America.* New York: Oxford University Press, 1985.

Hall, Donald, ed. *The Oxford Illustrated Book of American Children's Poems.* New York: Oxford University Press, 1999.

Larrick, Nancy. *Piping down the Valleys Wild: Poetry for the Young of All Ages.* Illus. by Ellen Raskin. New York: Bantam Doubleday Dell Books for Young Readers, 1999.

Philip, Neil, ed. *The New Oxford Book of Children's Verse.* Oxford: Oxford University Press, 1996.

Prelutsky, Jack, ed. *The Random House Book of Poetry for Children.* Illus. by Arnold Lobel. New York: Random House, 1983.

Sword, Elizabeth Hauge, and Victoria McCarthy, eds. *A Child's Anthology of Poetry.* Illus. by Tom Pohrt. Hopewell, NJ: Ecco, 1995.

"We Real Cool"   —*Gwendolyn Brooks*

First lines: "We real cool. We / left school"

This poem can be found in the following:
Ciardi, John. *How Does a Poem Mean?* Boston: Houghton Mifflin, 1960.
Kennedy, X. J., and Dorothy M. Kennedy. *Knock at a Star: A Child's Introduction to Poetry.* Illus. by Karen Ann Weinhaus. Boston: Little, Brown, 1982.

"The Sun Is Stuck"   —*Myra Cohn Livingston*

First lines: "The sun is stuck. / I mean, it won't move"

This poem can be found in the following:
Livingston, Myra Cohn. *A Song I Sang to You: A Selection of Poems.* Illus. by Margot Tomes. San Diego: Harcourt Brace Jovanovich, 1984.

Thoughts for Growing

"Someone's Face"   —*John Ciardi*

First line: "Someone's face was all frowned shut"

This poem can be found in the following:
Ciardi, John. *The Man Who Sang the Sillies.* Illus. by Edward Gorey. Philadelphia: Lippincott, 1961.

Prelutsky, Jack, ed. *Read-Aloud Rhymes for the Very Young.* Illus. by Marc Brown. New York: Knopf, 1986.

"Smiles Are Catchy"   —*Anon.*

Smiles are catchy
Like measles they say
Better watch out
I have one today.

Smiles are catchy
And so I suppose,
One might pop out
Right under your nose!

"Don't Worry"   —*Anon.*
Don't worry if your job is small,
And your rewards are few.
Remember that the mighty oak
Was once a nut like you.

"My—Oh Wow!—Book"   —*Judith Viorst*

First lines: "I'm lying here / and I'm sick in bed"

This poem can be found in the following:
Viorst, Judith. *If I Were in Charge of the World: And Other Worries.* New York: Aladdin, 1981.

"However They Talk"   —*Anon.*
However they talk, whatever they say
Look straight at the task without dismay.
And if you can do it, do it today.

"If I Can Stop One Heart from Breaking 'Not in Vain'"   —*Emily Dickinson*

First line: "If I can stop one heart from breaking"

This poem can be found in the following:
Dickinson, Emily. *The Complete Poems of Emily Dickinson.* Boston: Little, Brown, 1960.

"To Have Nothing at All Is to Have Much Still" —*Elizabeth Coatsworth*

First line: "To have nothing at all is to have much still"

This poem can be found in the following:
> Coatsworth, Elizabeth Jane. *The Fair American.* Illus. by Helen Sewell. New York: Macmillan, 1940.

"Ten Kinds" —*Mary Mapes Dodge*

First line: "Whinney Whiney, all things grieve her"

This poem can be found in the following:
> Prelutsky, Jack, ed. *The Random House Book of Poetry for Children.* Illus. by Arnold Lobel. New York: Random House, 1983.

"Kind Hearts are Gardens" —*Anon.*

Kind hearts are gardens
Kind thoughts are roots
Kind words are blossoms
Kind deeds are fruits.

"Against Idleness and Mischief" —*Isaac Watts*

How doth the little busy Bee
Improve each shining Hour,
And gather Honey all the day
From every opening Flower!

How skilfully she builds her Cell!
How neat she spreads the Wax!
And labours hard to store it well
With the sweet Food she makes.

In Works of Labour or of Skill
I would be busy too:
For Satan finds some Mischief still
For idle Hands to do.

In Books, or Work, or healthful Play
Let my first Years be past,
That I may give for every Day
Some good Account at last.

This poem can be found in the following:
   Ciardi, John. *How Does a Poem Mean?* Boston: Houghton Mifflin, 1960.

"Stick to Your Task"   —*Anon.*

   Stick to your task
   Till it sticks to you
   Beginners are many
   But enders are few.

   Honor, power, place and praise.
   Will come in the time of him who stays.

   Stick to the task
   Till it sticks to you
   Bend at it, sweat at it, smile at it, too.

   For out of the bend, the sweat and the smile
   Will come life's victories after a while.

"Learning"   —*Judith Viorst*

First line: "I'm learning to say thank you"

This poem can be found in the following:
   Poets.org, at www.poets.org/poetsorg/poem/learning.

"Routine"   —*Arthur Guiterman*

First lines: "No matter what we are and who, / Some duties everyone must do"

This poem can be found in the following:
   Keillor, Garrison. *Good Poems.* New York: Viking, 2002.
   Prelutsky, Jack, ed. *The Random House Book of Poetry for Children.* Illus. by
      Arnold Lobel. New York: Random House, 1983.

"Dreams"   —*Langston Hughes*

First line: "Hold fast to dreams"
This poem can be found in the following:
   Poemhunter.com, at www.poemhunter.com/poem/dreams-2.

"Some Thoughts from Arthur Guiterman: —*Arthur Guiterman*
Of Quarrels"

First line: "When eagles fight with raging hearts"

This poem can be found in the following:
> Arbuthnot, May Hill, and Shelton L. Root, eds. *Time for Poetry: A Representative Collection of Poetry for Children, to Be Used in the Classroom, Home, or Camp; Especially Planned for College Classes in Children's Literature.* Illus. by Arthur Paul. Glenview, IL: Scott, Foresman, 1967.

"Good Advice (of Counsel)"   —*Arthur Guiterman*

First line: "Who takes Advice of Each and Everyone"

This poem can be found in the following:
> "A Poet's Proverbs: Being Mirthful, Sober, and Fanciful Epigrams on the Universe, with Certain Old Irish Proverbs, All in Rhymed Complets," at www.amazon.com/poets-proverbs-mirthful-fanciful-epigrams/dp/ B00086L82K/ref=sr_1_1?s=books&ie=UTF8&qid=1362869135& sr=1–1&keywords=poet%27s+proverbs+guiterman.

Other Guiterman poems you might wish to use:
> "Short Sermon"
> "William the Testy"
> "Poem on the Spring?"
> "Of Courtesy"
> "Lesson from a Sundial"

Another source for the Guiterman poems:
> Guiterman, Arthur. *Ballads of Old New York.* Illus. by Scott Williams. New York; London: Harper and Brothers, 1920. http://name.umdl .umich.edu/ABB0654.

"The Plant Cut Down to the Root"   —*Elizabeth Coatsworth*

First lines: "The plant cut down to the root / does not hate"

This poem can be found in the following:
> Coatsworth, Elizabeth Jane. *The Fair American.* Illus. by Helen Sewell. New York: Macmillan, 1940.

"Two Friends"   —*David Ignatow*

First line: "I have something to tell you"

This poem can be found in the following:

> Dore, Anita. *The Premier Book of Major Poets: An Anthology.* New York: Fawcett Columbine, 1996.
>
> Ignatow, David. *Against the Evidence: Selected Poems, 1934–1994.* Middletown, CT: Wesleyan University Press, 1993.

"Mercy," from *The Merchant of Venice*   —*William Shakespeare*

> The quality of mercy is not strained;
> It droppeth as the gentle rain from heaven
> Upon the place beneath: It is twice blest,—
> It blesseth him that gives and him that takes:
> 'Tis mightiest in the mightiest; It becomes
> The throned monarch better than his crown:
> His sceptre shows the force of temporal power,
> The attribute to awe and majesty,
> Wherein doth sit the dread and fear of kings;
> But mercy is above the sceptred sway;—
> It is enthroned in the hearts of kings,
> It is an attribute to God Himself;
> And earthly power doth then show likest God's,
> When mercy seasons justice.

"Polonius' Advice to Laertes," from *Hamlet*   —*William Shakespeare*

> "There,—my blessing with you!
> And these few precepts in your memory
> See thou character.—Give thy thoughts no tongue,
> Nor any unproportion'd thought his act.
> Be thou familiar, but by no means vulgar.
> The friends thou hasts, and their adoption tried,
> Grapple them to thy soul with hoops of steel;
> Of each new-hatched, unfledged comrade. Beware
> Of entrance to a quarrel; but being in,
> Bear't that the opposed may beware of thee.
> Give every man thine ear, but few thy voice:
> Take each man's censure, but reserve thy judgement.
> Costly thy habit as purse can buy,

But not expressed in fancy; rich, not gaudy:
For the apparel oft proclaims the man.
Neither a borrower or a lender be,
For loan oft loses both itself and friend,
And borrowing dulls the edge of husbandry.
This above all: To thine own self be true.
And it must follow, as the night the day,
Thou canst' not then be false to any man."

Words and Books

"A Word Is Dead"
—*Emily Dickinson*

A word is dead
When it is said,
Some say.
I say it just
Begins to live
That day.

This poem can be found in the following:

Kennedy, X. J., and Dorothy M. Kennedy. *Knock at a Star: A Child's Introduction to Poetry.* Illus. by Karen Ann Weinhaus. Boston: Little, Brown, 1982.

Prelutsky, Jack, ed. *The Random House Book of Poetry for Children.* Illus. by Arnold Lobel. New York: Random House, 1983.

"How to Eat a Poem"
—*Eve Merriam*

First line: "Don't be polite"

This poem can be found in the following:

Sword, Elizabeth Hauge, and Victoria McCarthy, eds. *A Child's Anthology of Poetry.* Illus. by Tom Pohrt. Hopewell, NJ: Ecco, 1995.

"Sometimes Poems Are"
—*Judith Viorst*

First lines: "Sometimes poems are / short and fat"

This poem can be found in the following:

Viorst, Judith. *If I Were in Charge of the World: And Other Worries.* New York: Aladdin, 1981.

"The Library"

—*Barbara A. Huff*

It looks like any building
When you pass it on the street,
Made of stone and glass and marble,
Made of iron and concrete.

But once inside you can ride
A camel or a train,
Visit Rome, Siam, or Nome,
Feel a hurricane,

Meet a king, learn to sing,
How to bake a pie,
Go to sea, plant a tree,
Find how airplanes fly,

Train a horse, and of course
Have all the dogs you'd like,
See the moon, a sandy dune,
Or catch a whopping pike.

Everything that books can bring
You'll find inside those walls.
A world is there for you to share
When adventure calls.

You cannot tell its magic
By the way the building looks,
But there's wonderment within it,
The wonderment of books.

This poem can be found in the following:

Ferris, Helen Josephine. *Favorite Poems: Old and New.* Illus. by Leonard
    Weisgard. Garden City, NY: Doubleday, 1957.
Prelutsky, Jack, ed. *The Random House Book of Poetry for Children.* Illus. by
    Arnold Lobel. New York: Random House, 1983.

"Poetry"

—*Eleanor Farjeon*

First line: "What is Poetry? Who knows?"

This poem can be found in the following:

Farjeon, Eleanor. *Eleanor Farjeon's Poems for Children.* Philadelphia: Lippin-
    cott, 1951.

Prelutsky, Jack, ed. *The Random House Book of Poetry for Children.* Illus. by Arnold Lobel. New York: Random House, 1983.

"Primer Lesson" —*Carl Sandburg*

Look out how you use proud words.
When you let proud words go, it is
not easy to call them back.
They wear long boots, hard boots; they
walk off proud; they can't hear you calling—
Look out how you use proud words.

This poem can be found in the following:
Sandburg, Carl. *The Complete Poems of Carl Sandburg.* New York: Harcourt Brace Jovanovich, 1970.

"Feelings about Words" —*Mary O'Neill*

First line: "Some words clink"

This poem can be found in the following:
Prelutsky, Jack, ed. *The Random House Book of Poetry for Children.* Illus. by Arnold Lobel. New York: Random House, 1983.

Holiday Poems: Halloween

"Skeleton Parade" —*Jack Prelutsky*

First line: "The skeletons are out tonight"

This poem can be found in the following:
Cole, Joanna. *A New Treasury of Children's Poetry: Old Favorites and New Discoveries.* Illus. by Judith Gwyn Brown. Garden City, NY: Doubleday, 1984.
Prelutsky, Jack, ed. *Read-Aloud Rhymes for the Very Young.* Illus. by Marc Brown. New York: Knopf, 1986.

"On the Wiggley-Woggley Men" —*Spike Milligan*

On the wiggley-woggley men
The don't get up till ten
They run about
Then give a shout
And back to bed again.

"The Witch of Willoughby Wood"   —*Rowena Bennett*

First line: "There once was a witch of Willoughby Wood"

This poem can be found in the following:

de Regniers, Beatrice Schenk, ed. *Sing a Song of Popcorn: Every Child's Book of Poems.* Illus. by Marcia Brown. New York: Scholastic, 1988.

Sword, Elizabeth Hauge, and Victoria McCarthy, eds. *A Child's Anthology of Poetry.* Illus. by Tom Pohrt. Hopewell, NJ: Ecco, 1995.

"Night Comes"   —*Beatrice Schenk de Regniers*

First lines: "Night comes / leaking/out of the sky"

This poem can be found in the following:

Prelutsky, Jack, ed. *The Random House Book of Poetry for Children.* Illus. by Arnold Lobel. New York: Random House, 1983.

Prelutsky, Jack, ed. *Read-Aloud Rhymes for the Very Young.* Illus. by Marc Brown. New York: Knopf, 1986.

"The Spangled Pandemonium"   —*Palmer Brown*

First lines: "The Spangled Pandemonium / Is missing from the zoo"

This poem can be found in the following:

Arbuthnot, May Hill, and Shelton L. Root, eds. *Time for Poetry: A Representative Collection of Poetry for Children, to Be Used in the Classroom, Home, or Camp; Especially Planned for College Classes in Children's Literature.* Illus. by Arthur Paul. Glenview, IL: Scott, Foresman, 1967.

Fisher, Robert. *Amazing Monsters: Verses to Thrill and Chill.* Illus. by Rowena Allen. London: Faber and Faber, 1982.

Prelutsky, Jack, ed. *The Random House Book of Poetry for Children.* Illus. by Arnold Lobel. New York: Random House, 1983.

"Little Orphant Annie"   —*James Whitcomb Riley*

LITTLE Orphant Annie's come to our house to stay,
An' wash the cups an' saucers up, an' brush the crumbs away,
An' shoo the chickens off the porch, an' dust the hearth, an' sweep,
An' make the fire, an' bake the bread, an' earn her board-an'-keep;

An' all us other childern, when the supper-things is done,
We set around the kitchen fire an' has the mostest fun
A-list'nin' to the witch-tales 'at Annie tells about,
An' the Gobble-uns 'at gits you

Ef you
Don't
Watch
Out!

Wunst they wuz a little boy wouldn't say his prayers,—
An' when he went to bed at night, away up-stairs,
His Mammy heerd him holler, an' his Daddy heerd him bawl,
An' when they turn't the kivvers down, he wuzn't there at all!

An' they seeked him in the rafter-room, an' cubby-hole, an' press,
An' seeked him up the chimbly-flue, an' ever'-wheres, I guess;
But all they ever found wuz thist his pants an' roundabout:—
An' the Gobble-uns'll git you
Ef you
Don't
Watch
Out!

An' one time a little girl 'ud allus laugh an' grin,
An' make fun of ever' one, an' all her blood-an'-kin;
An' wunst, when they was "company," an' ole folks wuz there,
She mocked 'em an' shocked 'em, an' said she didn't care!

An' thist as she kicked her heels, an' turn't to run an' hide,
They wuz two great big Black Things a-standin' by her side,
An' they snatched her through the ceilin' 'fore she knowed what she's
    about!
An' the Gobble-uns'll git you
Ef you
Don't
Watch
Out!

An' little Orphant Annie says, when the blaze is blue,
An' the lamp-wick sputters, an' the wind goes woo-oo!
An' you hear the crickets quit, an' the moon is gray,
An' the lightnin'-bugs in dew is all squenched away,—
You better mind yer parunts, an' yer teachurs fond an' dear,
An' churish them 'at loves you, an' dry the orphant's tear,
An' he'p the pore an' needy ones 'at clusters all about,
Er the Gobble-uns'll git you
Ef you
Don't
Watch
Out!

This poem can be found in the following:
> Riley, James Whitcomb. *The Complete Works of James Whitcomb Riley.* New York: Collier, 1916.

"There Aren't Any Ghosts" —*Judith Viorst*

> There aren't any ghosts,
> There aren't any.
> There aren't any gh—h—h . . . .
> Well—not too many.

"Something Is There" —*Lillian Moore*

First lines: "Something is there / there on the stair"

This poem can be found in the following:
> Livingston, Myra Cohn. *Why Am I Grown So Cold? Poems of the Unknowable.* New York: Atheneum, 1982.
> Prelutsky, Jack, ed. *The Random House Book of Poetry for Children.* Illus. by Arnold Lobel. New York: Random House, 1983.

"A Prayer for Halloween" —*Anon.*

> From ghoulies and ghosties,
> Long-leggety beasties,
> And things
> That go bump in the night,
> Good Lord, deliver us.

"This Is Halloween" —*Dorothy Brown Thompson*

First line: "Goblins on the doorstep"

This poem can be found in the following:
> Arbuthnot, May Hill, and Shelton L. Root, eds. *Time for Poetry: A Representative Collection of Poetry for Children, to Be Used in the Classroom, Home, or Camp; Especially Planned for College Classes in Children's Literature.* Illus. by Arthur Paul. Glenview, IL: Scott, Foresman, 1967.
> Prelutsky, Jack, ed. *The Random House Book of Poetry for Children.* Illus. by Arnold Lobel. New York: Random House, 1983.

"The Creature in the Classroom"   —*Jack Prelutsky*

First line: "It appeared inside our classroom"

This poem can be found in the following:
Prelutsky, Jack, ed. *The Random House Book of Poetry for Children.* Illus. by
Arnold Lobel. New York: Random House, 1983.

From "Witch's Broom Notes"   —*David McCord*

On Halloween, what bothers some
About these witches is, how come
In sailing through the air like bats
They never seem to lose their hats?

"What Night Would It Be?"   —*John Ciardi*

First lines: "If the moon shines / on the black pines"

This poem can be found in the following:
Larrick, Nancy. *Piping down the Valleys Wild: Poetry for the Young of All
Ages.* Illus. by Ellen Raskin. New York: Bantam Doubleday Dell Books
for Young Readers, 1999.

"The House at the Corner"   —*Myra Cohn Livingston*

First lines: "The house at the corner / is cold grey stone"

This poem can be found in the following:
Brown, Marc. *Scared Silly! A Book for the Brave.* Boston: Little, Brown,
1994.

"Father and Mother"   —*X. J. Kennedy*

First line: "My father's name is Frankenstein"

This poem can be found in the following:
Prelutsky, Jack, ed. *The Random House Book of Poetry for Children.* Illus. by
Arnold Lobel. New York: Random House, 1983.

"Tombstone"   —*Lucia M. Hymes and James L. Hymes Jr.*

First line: "Here lies a bully"

This poem can be found in the following:
Prelutsky, Jack, ed. *The Random House Book of Poetry for Children.* Illus. by
Arnold Lobel. New York: Random House, 1983.

"Song of the Witches," from *Macbeth*   —*William Shakespeare*

"Double, double, toil and trouble;
Fire burn and cauldron bubble.
Fillet of a fenny snake,
In the cauldron boil and bake;

Eye of newt and toe of frog,
Wool of bat and tongue of dog,
Adder's fork and blind-worm's sting,
Lizard's leg and howlet's wing,

For a charm of powerful trouble,
Like a hell-broth boil and bubble.
Double, double toil and trouble;
Fire burn and cauldron bubble.

Cool it with a baboon's blood,
Then the charm is firm and good."

Holiday Poems: Valentine's Day

"Valentine"   —*Shel Silverstein*

First line: "I got a valentine from…"

This poem can be found in the following:
Cole, William. *Poems for Seasons and Celebrations.* Illus. by Johannes
Troyer. Cleveland: World, 1961.
Prelutsky, Jack, ed. *The Random House Book of Poetry for Children.* Illus. by
Arnold Lobel. New York: Random House, 1983.

"Opposites" —*Richard Wilbur*

What is the opposite of two?
A lonely me, a lonely you

This poem can be found in the following:
Livingston, Myra Cohn. *I Like You, if You Like Me: Poems of Friendship.* New
York: Margaret K. McElderry, 1987.
Prelutsky, Jack, ed. *The Random House Book of Poetry for Children.* Illus. by
Arnold Lobel. New York: Random House, 1983.

"The Night Has a Thousand Eyes" —*Francis William Bourdillon*

The night has a thousand eyes,
  the day but one;
Yet the light of the bright world dies
with the dying sun.
The mind has a thousand eyes,
  and the heart but one;
Yet the light of a whole life dies
  then its love is done.

Holiday Poems: Thanksgiving

"The Turkey" —*Anon.*

He lay there on the table
That gobbler plump and round
And when it was time to cook it,
It was nowhere to be found.

We looked all through the kitchen
And through the pantry well
We asked Kate if she had seen it
And John and Annabelle.

And even tiny Mary,
We asked her if she knew
About the missing turkey
And she said, 'Why t'ourse, I do!

Po' to'key doesn't feel well
T'ause he lost his head.
So I put my nighty on him
And tucked him in my bed.'

From "Thanksgiving"   —Louise Driscoll

Thank you, God,
That swallows know their way
In the great sky;
That grass, all brown today,
And dead and dry,
Will quiver in the sun
All green and gay
When winter's done.

"Thanksgiving"   —*Margaret Hillert*

I feel so stuffed inside my skin
And full of little groans,
I know just how the turkey felt
Before it turned to bones.

"All Things Bright and Beautiful"   —*Cecil Frances Alexander*

All things bright and beautiful,
All creatures great and small,
All things wise and wonderful,
The Lord God made them all.

Each little flower that opens,
Each little bird that sings,
He made their glowing colours,
He made their tiny wings.

The purple-headed mountain,
The river running by,
The sunset, and the morning,
That brightens up the sky;

The cold wind in the winter,
The pleasant summer sun,
The ripe fruits in the garden,
He made them every one.

He gave us eyes to see them, And lips that we might tell, How great is God
  Almighty, Who has made all things well.

"We Thank Thee" —Ralph Waldo Emerson

For flowers that bloom about our feet;
For tender grass, so fresh, so sweet;
For song of bird, and hum of bee;
Father in Heaven, we thank thee.

For blue of stream and blue of sky;
For pleasant shade of branches high;
For fragrant air and cooling breeze;
For beauty of the blooming trees,

Father in Heaven we thank thee.

"He Who Has Never Known Hunger" —Elizabeth Coatsworth

First lines: "Who has never known hunger / has never known good"

This poem can be found in the following:
Arbuthnot, May Hill, and Shelton L. Root, eds. *Time for Poetry: A Representative Collection of Poetry for Children, to Be Used in the Classroom, Home, or Camp; Especially Planned for College Classes in Children's Literature.* Illus. by Arthur Paul. Glenview, IL: Scott, Foresman, 1967.

"Blessed Lord, What It Is to Be Young" —David McCord

First line: "Blessed Lord, what it is to be young"

This poem can be found in the following:
Cole, Joanna. *A New Treasury of Children's Poetry: Old Favorites and New Discoveries.* Illus. by Judith Gwyn Brown. Garden City, NY: Doubleday, 1984.
Kennedy, X. J., and Dorothy M. Kennedy. *Knock at a Star: A Child's Introduction to Poetry.* Illus. by Karen Ann Weinhaus. Boston: Little, Brown, 1982.

Holiday Poems: Christmas

"A Bundle Is a Funny Thing" —John Farrer

A bundle is a funny thing,
It always sets me wondering;
For whether it is thin or wide
You never know just what's inside.

Especially on Christmas week,
Temptation is so great to peek!
Now wouldn't it be much more fun
If shoppers carried things undone?

"Day before Christmas"   —*Marchette Chute*

First line: "We have been helping with the cake"

This poem can be found in the following:
> Cole, Joanna. *A New Treasury of Children's Poetry: Old Favorites and New
> Discoveries.* Illus. by Judith Gwyn Brown. Garden City, NY: Doubleday,
> 1984.
> Kennedy, X. J., and Dorothy M. Kennedy. *Knock at a Star: A Child's Intro-
> duction to Poetry.* Illus. by Karen Ann Weinhaus. Boston: Little, Brown,
> 1982.

"My Gift"   —*Christina G. Rossetti*

What can I give Him,
Poor as I am?
If I were a shepherd
I would bring a lamb,
If I were a Wise Man
I would do my part,—
Yet what I can I give Him,
Give my heart.

From "A Christmas Package VII"   —*David McCord*

First lines: "My stocking's where / We'll see it—there!"

This poem can be found in the following:
> Prelutsky, Jack, ed. *The Random House Book of Poetry for Children.* Illus. by
> Arnold Lobel. New York: Random House, 1983.

"Fir"   —*Joan Hanson*

First line: "Fir tree tall"

This poem can be found in the following:
> Beneduce, Ann Keay. *Joy to the World: A Family Christmas Treasury.* Illus.
> by Gennady Spirin. New York: Atheneum Books for Young Readers,
> 2000.

"Otto" —*Gwendolyn Brooks*

First lines: "It's Christmas day / I did not get / the presents I had hoped for. Yet"

This poem can be found in the following:

Larrick, Nancy. *Piping down the Valleys Wild: Poetry for the Young of All Ages.* Illus. by Ellen Raskin. New York: Bantam Doubleday Dell Books for Young Readers, 1999.

Livingston, Myra Cohn. *Poems of Christmas.* New York: Atheneum, 1980.

Prelutsky, Jack, ed. *The Random House Book of Poetry for Children.* Illus. by Arnold Lobel. New York: Random House, 1983.

"Christmas Bells"
or "I Heard the Bells on Christmas Day" —*Henry Wadsworth Longfellow*

I heard the bells on Christmas Day
Their old, familiar carols play,
And wild and sweet
The words repeat
Of peace on earth, good-will to men!

And thought how, as the day had come,
The belfries of all Christendom
Had rolled along
The unbroken song
Of peace on earth, good-will to men!

Till ringing, singing on its way,
The world revolved from night to day,
A voice, a chime,
A chant sublime
Of peace on earth, good-will to men!

Then from each black, accursed mouth
The cannon thundered in the South,
And with the sound
The carols drowned
Of peace on earth, good-will to men!

It was as if an earthquake rent
The hearth-stones of a continent,
And made forlorn
The households born
Of peace on earth, good-will to men!

And in despair I bowed my head;
"There is no peace on earth," I said,
"For hate is strong,
And mocks the song
Of peace on earth, good-will to men!"

Then pealed the bells more loud and deep:
"God is not dead, nor doth He sleep!
The Wrong shall fail,
The Right prevail,
With peace on earth, good-will to men!"

II. Fiction

Set 1

Aiken, Joan. *A Necklace of Raindrops.* Illus. by Jan Pieńkowski. London: Jonathan Cape, 2009.

Allsburg, Chris Van, author and illus. *The Garden of Abdul Gasazi.* Boston: Houghton Mifflin, 1979.

Atwater, Richard, and Florence Atwater. *Mr. Popper's Penguins.* Illus. by Robert Lawson. Boston: Little, Brown, 1988.

Brown, Margaret Wise. *The Important Book.* Illus. by Leonard Weisgard. New York: Harper, 1949.

Bulla, Clyde Robert. *Shoeshine Girl.* Illus. by Leigh Grant. New York: Crowell, 1975.

Carrick, Carol. *Old Mother Witch.* Illus. by Donald Carrick. New York: Seabury, 1975.

Caudill, Rebecca. *Did You Carry the Flag Today, Charlie?* Illus. by Nancy Grossman. New York: Holt, Rinehart and Winston, 1966.

Cleary, Beverly. *Ralph S. Mouse.* Illus. by Paul O. Zelinsky. New York: Morrow, 1982.

Cole, Babette. *The Hairy Book.* New York: Random House, 1985.

Coombs, Patricia. *Dorrie and the Haunted House.* New York: Lothrop, Lee, and Shepard, 1970.

Dahl, Roald. *The Magic Finger.* Illus. by William Pène Du Bois. New York: Harper and Row, 1966.

de Caylus, le comte, author, and Benjamin Appel, adapter. *Heart of Ice.* Illus. by J. K. Lambert. New York: Pantheon, 1977.

dePaola, Tomie. *Helga's Dowry: A Troll Love Story.* New York: Harcourt Brace Jovanovich, 1977.

Devlin, Wende. *Cranberry Thanksgiving.* Illus. by Harry Devlin. New York: Parents' Magazine, 1971.

Duncan, Jane. *Janet Reachfar and Chickabird.* Illus. by Mairi Hedderwick. New York: Seabury, 1978.

Estes, Eleanor. *The Hundred Dresses.* Illus. by Louis Slobodkin. New York: Harcourt, Brace and World, 1944.

Fleischman, Sid. *McBroom Tells the Truth.* Illus. by Kurt Werth. New York: Norton, 1966.

Flora, James. *Grandpa's Ghost Stories: Story and Pictures.* New York: Atheneum, 1978.

Galdone, Joanna. *The Tailypo: A Ghost Story.* Illus. by Paul Galdone. New York: Seabury, 1977.

Gerrard, Roy. *Sir Cedric.* New York: Farrar, Straus and Giroux, 1984.

Griffith, Helen V. *Alex and the Cat.* Illus. by Joseph Low. New York: Greenwillow, 1982.

Griffith, Helen V. *More Alex and the Cat.* Illus. by Donald Carrick. New York: Greenwillow, 1983.

Hoban, Russell. *The Sorely Trying Day.* Illus. by Lillian Hoban. New York: Harper and Row, 1964.

Jonas, Ann. *Round Trip.* New York: Greenwillow, 1983.

Kennedy, Richard. *The Contests at Cowlick.* Illus. by Marc Simont. Boston: Little, Brown, 1975.

Kennedy, Richard, and Ronald Himler. *Inside My Feet: The Story of a Giant.* New York: Harper and Row, 1979.

Laurin, Anne. *Little Things.* Illus. by Marcia Sewall. New York: Atheneum, 1978.

MacDonald, Betty Bard. *Mrs. Piggle-Wiggle.* Illus. by Richard Bennett. Philadelphia: Lippincott, 1947.

Manushkin, Fran. *Baby, Come Out!* Illus. by Ronald Himler. New York: Star Bright, 2002.

Marshall, James. *Yummers!* Boston: Houghton Mifflin, 1972.

Massie, Diane Redfield. *Chameleon Was a Spy.* New York: Crowell, 1979.

Mayer, Mercer. *A Special Trick.* New York: Dial, 1970.

McCloskey, Robert. *Lentil.* New York: Viking, 1940.

McDonnell, Christine. *Toad Food & Measle Soup.* Illus. by G. Brian Karas. New York: Viking, 2001.

Meyer, Franklyn E. *Me and Caleb.* Illus. by Lawrence Beall Smith. Chicago: Follett, 1962.

Moeri, Louise. *Star Mother's Youngest Child.* Illus. by Trina Schart Hyman. Boston: Houghton Mifflin, 1975.

Peterson, Jeanne Whitehouse. *I Have a Sister, My Sister Is Deaf.* New York: Harper and Row, 1984.

Peterson, John Lawrence. *The Littles.* Illus. by Roberta Carter Clark. New York: Scholastic, 1967.

Raskin, Ellen. *Spectacles.* New York: Atheneum, 1968.

Rayner, Mary. *Mrs. Pig's Bulk Buy.* New York: Atheneum, 1981.

Seuss, Dr. *The Butter Battle Book.* New York: Random House, 1984.

Sharmat, Marjorie Weinman. *Gila Monsters Meet You at the Airport.* Illus. by Byron Barton. New York: Macmillan, 1980.

Sharmat, Mitchell. *Gregory, the Terrible Eater.* Illus. by Jose Aruego and Ariane Dewey. New York: Four Winds, 1980.

Silverstein, Shel, author and illus. *Lafcadio: The Lion Who Shot Back.* New York: Harper, 1963.

Viorst, Judith. *The Tenth Good Thing about Barney.* Illus. by Erik Blegvad. New York: Atheneum, 1971.

Wangerin, Walter. *Thistle.* Illus. by Marcia Sewall. New York: Harper and Row, 1983.

White, E. B. *Stuart Little.* Illus. by Garth Williams. New York: Harper and Row, 1973.

Williams, Vera B. *A Chair for My Mother.* New York: Greenwillow, 1982.

Williams, Vera B. *Something Special for Me.* New York: Greenwillow, 1983.

Yorinks, Arthur, and Cynthia Krupat. *It Happened in Pinsk.* Illus. by Richard Egielski. New York: Farrar, Straus and Giroux, 1983.

Zemach, Harve. *The Judge: An Untrue Tale.* Illus. by Margot Zemach. New York: Farrar, Straus and Giroux, 1969.

Set 2

Aliki. *A Medieval Feast.* New York: Thomas Y. Crowell, 1983.

Blume, Judy. *Superfudge.* New York: Dutton, 1980.

Blume, Judy. *Tales of a Fourth Grade Nothing.* Illus. by Roy Doty. New York: Dutton, 1972.

Bulla, Clyde Robert. *The Sword in the Tree.* Illus. by Bruce Bowles. New York: HarperCollins World, 2000.

Gilson, Jamie. *Thirteen Ways to Sink a Sub.* Illus. by Linda Edwards. New York: Lothrop, Lee and Shepard, 1982.

Greer, Gery, and Bob Ruddick. *Max and Me and the Time Machine.* San Diego: Harcourt Brace Jovanovich, 1983.

Lewis, C. S. *The Lion, the Witch, and the Wardrobe.* Illus. by Pauline Baynes. New York: HarperCollins, 1994.

Morey, Walt. *Gentle Ben.* Illus. by John Schoenherr. New York: Dutton, 1965.

Peck, Robert Newton. *Soup.* Illus. by Charles C. Gehm. New York: Knopf, 1974.

Reyher, Rebecca Hourwich, and Ruth Chrisman Gannett. *My Mother Is the Most Beautiful Woman in the World: A Russian Folktale.* Boston: Lothrop, Lee and Shepard, 1945.

Robinson, Barbara. *The Best Christmas Pageant Ever.* Illus. by Judith Gwyn Brown. New York: Harper and Row, 1972.

Seredy, Kate. *A Tree for Peter.* New York: Viking, 1941.

Shreve, Susan Richards. *The Flunking of Joshua T. Bates.* Illus. by Diane De Groat. New York: Knopf, 1984.

Sperry, Armstrong. *Call It Courage.* New York: Macmillan, 1940.

Set 3

Alexander, Lloyd. *The Book of Three.* New York: Holt, Rinehart and Winston, 1964.

Banks, Lynne Reid. *The Indian in the Cupboard.* Illus. by Brock Cole. Garden City, NY: Doubleday, 1980.

Bellairs, John. *The House with a Clock in Its Walls.* Illus. by Edward Gorey. New York: Dial, 1973.

Bishop, Claire Huchet. *Twenty and Ten.* Illus. by William Pène du Bois. New York: Viking, 1952.

Edmonds, Walter Dumaux. *The Matchlock Gun.* Illus. by Paul Lantz. New York: Dodd, Mead, 1941.

Fitzgerald, John Dennis. *The Great Brain.* Illus. by Mercer Mayer. New York: Dial, 1967.

Forbes, Esther. *Johnny Tremain: A Novel for Old and Young.* Illus. by Lynd Ward. Boston: Houghton Mifflin, 1943.

Howe, Deborah, and James Howe. *Bunnicula: A Rabbit Tale of Mystery.* Illus. by Alan Daniel. New York: Atheneum, 1979.

Hughes, Dean. *Honestly, Myron.* New York: Atheneum, 1982.

Key, Alexander. *The Forgotten Door.* Philadelphia: Westminster, 1965.

Lindgren, Astrid. *Ronia, the Robber's Daughter.* New York: Viking, 1983.

Peck, Richard. *The Ghost Belonged to Me: A Novel.* New York: Viking, 1975.

Peck, Richard. *Ghosts I Have Been: A Novel.* New York: Viking, 1977.

Sherman, D. R. *The Lion's Paw.* Garden City, NY: Doubleday, 1975.

Smith, Doris Buchanan. *A Taste of Blackberries.* Illus. by Charles Robinson. New York: Crowell, 1973.

Speare, Elizabeth George. *The Witch of Blackbird Pond.* Boston: Houghton Mifflin, 1958.

Taylor, Theodore. *The Cay.* Garden City, NY: Doubleday, 1969.

Taylor, Theodore. *Teetoncey*. Illus. by Richard Cuffari. Garden City, NY: Doubleday, 1974.

Yates, Elizabeth. *Amos Fortune: Free Man*. Illus. by Nora S. Unwin. New York: Dutton, 1950.

Set 4

Armstrong, William H. *Sour Land*. New York: Harper and Row, 1971.

Babbitt, Natalie. *Tuck Everlasting*. New York: Farrar, Straus and Giroux, 1975.

Christopher, John. *The White Mountains*. New York: Macmillan, 1967.

Cleary, Beverly. *Dear Mr. Henshaw*. Illus. by Paul O. Zelinsky. New York: Morrow, 1983.

Cooper, Susan. *The Dark Is Rising*. Illus. by Alan E. Cober. New York: Atheneum, 1973.

Creswick, Paul. *Robin Hood*. Illus. by N. C. Wyeth. New York: Scribner, 1984.

Crossley-Holland, Kevin, trans. *Beowulf*. New York: Farrar, Straus and Giroux, 1968.

Dahl, Roald. *The Witches*. Illus. by Quentin Blake. New York: Farrar, Straus and Giroux, 1983.

D'Aulaire, Ingri, and Edgar Parin D'Aulaire. *Ingri and Edgar Parin D'Aulaire's Book of Greek Myths*. Garden City, NY: Doubleday, 1962.

French, Harry W. *The Lance of Kanana*. Lothrop, Lee and Shepard, 1920.

George, Jean Craighead. *Julie of the Wolves*. Illus. by John Schoenherr. New York: Harper and Row, 1972.

Gilbert, Henry. *Robin Hood*. Illus. by Garth Williams. Philadelphia: Lippincott, 1948.

Hawthorne, Nathaniel. *A Wonder Book*. London: Dent, 1949.

Holm, Anne. *North to Freedom*. New York: Harcourt, Brace and World, 1965.

Jones, Diana Wynne. *Dogsbody*. New York: Greenwillow, 1977.

Kingsley, Charles. *The Heroes; or, Greek Fairy Tales for My Children*. Illus. by Maud Hunt Squire and E. Mars. New York: Schocken, 1970.

L'Engle, Madeleine. *A Wrinkle in Time*. New York: Farrar, Straus and Giroux, 1962.

Malam, John. *Jason and the Argonauts*. Illus. by David Antram. Minneapolis, MN: Picture Window, 2005.

McCaughrean, Geraldine. *Gilgamesh*. Illus. by David Parkins. Grand Rapids, MI: Eerdmans Books for Young Readers, 2003.

McCaughrean, Geraldine. *Theseus.* Chicago: Cricket, 2005.

McKinley, Robin. *Beauty: A Retelling of the Story of Beauty & the Beast.* New York: HarperCollins, 1978.

Osborne, Will, and Mary Pope Osborne. *Jason and the Argonauts.* Illus. by Steve Sullivan. New York: Scholastic, 1988.

Peck, Robert Newton. *A Day No Pigs Would Die.* New York: Knopf, 1972.

Schwartz, Alvin. *Scary Stories to Tell in the Dark.* Illus. by Stephen Gammell. New York: Lippincott, 1981.

Sebestyen, Ouida. *Words by Heart.* Boston: Little, Brown, 1979.

Singer, Isaac Bashevis. *Zlateh the Goat, and Other Stories.* Illus. by Maurice Sendak. New York: Harper and Row, 1966.

Slote, Alfred. *Hang Tough, Paul Mather.* Philadelphia: Lippincott, 1973.

Sutcliff, Rosemary. *Beowulf.* New York: Dutton, 1962.

Meet the Authors

Here is a list of authors to whom children ought to be introduced. You could build a program around any one of them.

- Beverly Cleary
- Eleanor Estes
- Donald Sobol
- Lloyd Alexander
- Jean Craighead George
- Betsy Byars
- William Armstrong
- Carol Ryrie Brink
- Bette Greene
- Virginia Hamilton
- Marguerite Henry
- Scott O'Dell
- Susan Cooper
- Katherine Paterson
- Louisa May Alcott
- Natalie Babbitt
- Madeline L'Engle
- Edgar Allen Poe
- Mark Twain
- Isaac Bashevis Singer

III. Folktales and Fairy Stories

Aardema, Verna, and Howard True Wheeler. *The Riddle of the Drum: A Tale from Tizapán, Mexico.* Illus. by Tony Chen. New York: Four Winds, 1979.

Aesop, and Jerry Pinkney. *Aesop's Fables.* New York: SeaStar, 2000.

Bang, Molly. *Dawn.* Illus. by G. G Laurens. New York: Morrow, 1983.

Bang, Molly. *Tye May and the Magic Brush.* New York: Greenwillow, 1981.

Black, Holly. *White Cat.* New York: Margaret K. McElderry, 2010.

Chase, Richard, R. M. Ward, and Herbert Halpert. *The Jack Tales.* Illus. by Berkeley Williams. Boston: Houghton Mifflin, 1943.

D'Aulaire, Ingri, and Edgar Parin D'Aulaire. *D'Aulaires' Trolls.* Garden City, NY: Doubleday, 1972.

Demi. *Liang and the Magic Paintbrush.* New York: Holt, 1993.

dePaola, Tomie. *Fin M'Coul: The Giant of Knockmany Hill.* New York: Trumpet Club, 1992.

Ginsburg, Mirra, and Douglas Florian. *The Night It Rained Pancakes: Adapted from a Russian Folktale.* New York: Greenwillow, 1980.

Goble, Paul. *The Gift of the Sacred Dog: Story and Illustrations.* Scarsdale, NY: Bradbury, 1980.

Grimm, Jacob, and Marguerite De Angeli. *The Goose Girl.* Garden City, NY: Doubleday, 1964.

Gurvin, Abe. *The Husband Who Was to Mind the House.* New York: Young Readers, 1968.

Hale, Shannon. *The Goose Girl.* New York: Bloomsbury, 2003.

Hogrogian, Nonny, Jacob Grimm, and Wilhelm Grimm. *The Devil with the Three Golden Hairs: A Tale from the Brothers Grimm.* New York: Knopf, 1983.

Kellogg, Steven. *Mike Fink: A Tall Tale.* New York: Morrow Junior Books, 1992.

Kennedy, Richard. *The Leprechaun's Story.* Illus. by Marcia Sewall. New York: Dutton, 1979.

Lobel, Arnold. *Ming Lo Moves the Mountain.* New York: Greenwillow, 1982.

Louie, Ai-Ling. *Yeh-Shen: A Cinderella Story from China.* Illus. by Ed Young. New York: Philomel, 1982.

Mayer, Marianna. *The Twelve Dancing Princesses.* Illus. by Kinuko Craft. New York: Morrow Junior Books, 1989.

Mayer, Mercer. *East of the Sun and West of the Moon.* New York: Four Winds, 1980.

McVitty, Walter, trans. *Ali Baba and the Forty Thieves.* Illus. by Margaret Early. New York: Abrams, 1989.

Mosel, Arlene. *The Funny Little Woman.* Illus. by Blair Lent. New York: Dutton, 1972.

Ransome, Arthur. *The Fool of the World and the Flying Ship: A Russian Tale.* Illus. by Uri Shulevitz. New York: Farrar, Straus and Giroux, 1968.

Raschka, Christopher. *Peter and the Wolf.* New York: Atheneum Books for Young Readers, 2008.

Rogasky, Barbara, Jacob Grimm, and Wilhelm Grimm. *Rapunzel.* Illus. by Trina Schart Hyman. New York: Holiday House, 1982.

Rounds, Glen. *Mr. Yowder and the Giant Bull Snake.* New York: Holiday House, 1978.

San Souci, Robert D. *The Legend of Scarface: A Blackfeet Indian Tale.* Illus. by Daniel San Souci. Garden City, NY: Doubleday, 1978.

Shapiro, Irwin. *Pecos Bill and Other Tales.* Illus. by Al Schmidt. New York: Golden, 1958.

Stevens, John. *Rapunzel.* Illus. by Paul O. Zelinsky and Amy Beniker. New York: Dutton Children's Books, 1997.

Yolen, Jane. *The Seeing Stick.* Illus. by Remy Charlip and Demetra Maraslis. New York: Thomas Y. Crowell, 1977.

Zemach, Harve. *Duffy and the Devil.* Illus. by Margot Zemach. New York: Farrar, Straus and Giroux, 1973.

IV. After-School Programs

Program Template

- Program Outline
- Program Title
- Topic
- Target Audience
- Ideal Audience Size
- Length of Program
- Setup Time
- Preprogram Time
- Goals and Objectives for This Specific Program
- Materials
- Books Read or Presented
- Poetry to Share
- Activities, Crafts, Games, and Source for Each
- Media Used and Source for Each
- Supplies Needed
- Extra Staff Needed
- Equipment Needed
- Room Setup
- Corresponding Exhibit or Display
- Contingency Plans
- Program Planning Calendar (see figure 3.1 for a blank calendar)

Figure 3.1 **Program Planning Calendar**

Program Title: _____

Week	Read-Aloud Chapters	Story Events	Brief Discussion	Activity	Materials and Supplies to Prepare
1					
2					
3					
4					
5					

Sample Programs

Figure 3.2 outlines an after-school program with various topics covered over an entire school year.

Figure 3.2 **School Yearlong Programming Outline**

Time frame	Topics	Books and Media	Poetry Themes	Authors	Activities
Nov.	Introduction Historical Fiction	*Sadako and the Thousand Paper Cranes*	Food/ Thanksgiving	Jean Fritz	Fold paper cranes Photography class
Dec. 1 – Jan. 21	Poetry Fables	Christmas stories DVDs: *Walrus and the Carpenter, Dead Ends and New Dreams*	Poems about poetry Christmas/ Winter/ New Year's Limericks	Arnold Lobel	Creative dramatization of *Fables* by Arnold Lobel Christmas crafts
Jan. 25 – Mar. 4	Realistic Fiction	*Twenty and Ten* DVDs: *Shoeshine Girl, Hug Me*	I Love You/ Valentine's Day Black History Month People and Things	Virginia Hamilton	Valentine craft
Mar. 7 – Apr. 20	Children's Classics	*The Whipping Boy* Film: *Adventures of J. Thaddeus Toad*	Classics	Beverly Cleary L. Frank Baum	Beverly Cleary birthday party

Sample Program Theme: Mysteries

The outline below illustrates a program held for ten weeks during the fall and highlighting mysteries. Use it to help get your thoughts and imagination going to plan your own mystery-themed series.

9/26   *Encyclopedia Brown and the Case of the Disgusting Sneakers*—Donald Sobol

10/3   *The Dollhouse Murders*—Betty Ren Wright

10/10   *Bad Day at Riverbend*—Chris Van Allsburg

10/17   "The Mystery of the Seven Wrong Clocks," from A*lfred Hitchcock's "Solve-Them-Yourself" Mysteries*

10/24   *The Eleventh Hour*—Graeme Base

11/14   *Shortcut* and *Black and White*—David Macaulay

11/21   *Who Killed Cock Robin?*—Jean Craighead George and *Piggins*—Jane Yolen

11/28   *Maurice Sendak's Christmas Mystery*—Maurice Sendak

Sample Program Theme: Fantasy

Use the ideas in figure 3.3 as a starting point for a series of programs highlighting fantasy. These ideas were quite successful and should spark your own ideas.

Figure 3.3 **Fantasy After-School Program**

Story or Book	Activities	Equipment Needed
"Utensile Strength," from *Book of Enchantments*—Patricia C. Wrede	Show children various common kitchen utensils and have them ascribe magical powers to them, just like the frying pan of doom in the story. How about the "fork of fear"?	Kitchen utensils, including the "Frying Pan of Doom"
Stories from *Tales from the Brothers Grimm and the Sisters Weird*—Vivian Vande Velde "All Points Bulletin"—Red Riding Hood *"And Now a Word from Our Sponsor"—commercials based on fairy tales	Have the children create their own fairy-tale advertisements.	Children's imaginations
The Magician's Boy—Susan Cooper Note: Because of the number of fairy tales, nursery rhymes, and other mythic stories incorporated in this book, it could be an entire program unto itself, culminating with a performance.	Watch a piece from *The Magician's Boy* (The Night Kitchen Radio Theater, Kennedy Center), at www.kennedy-center .org/explorer/artists/?entity _id=14977&source_type=B. Create a script from the book and perform it with the children. You can also use puppets.	

Figure 3.3 suggests activities involving Susan Cooper's *The Magician's Boy*. For poetry with Cooper's *The Magician's Boy*, use Mother Goose nursery rhymes. Revisit these and read favorites, individually and as a group.

As Merlin is a very important character in *The Magician's Boy*, the following poem might be useful.

"Merlin"   *—Edwin Muir*

> O Merlin in your crystal cave
> Deep in the diamond of the day,
> Will there ever be a singer
> Whose music will smooth away
> The furrow drawn by Adam's finger
> Across the memory and the wave?
> Or a runner who'll outrun
> Man's long shadow driving on,
> Break through the gate of memory
> And hang the apple on the tree?
> Will your magic ever show
> The sleeping bride shut in her bower,
> The day wreathed in its mound of snow
> and Time locked in his tower?

This poem can be found in the following:
    Poemhunter, at www.poemhunter.com/poem/merlin.

Other poems that connect with the themes of Susan Cooper's most famous work, *The Dark Is Rising Sequence,* follow:

"In a Dark Time"   *—Theodore Roethke*

First line: "In a dark time, the eye begins to see"

This poem can be found in the following:
    Roethke, Theodore. *The Collected Poems of Theodore Roethke.* Garden City,
        NY: Anchor, 1975.

"Windsor Forest—Herne's Oak"   *—William Shakespeare*
from The Merry Wives of Windsor

> There is an old tale goes, that Herne the hunter,
> Sometime a keeper here in Windsor Forest,

Doth all the winter time, at still midnight,
Walk round about an oak, with great ragg'd horns;
And there he blasts the tree, and takes the cattle;
And makes milch-kine yield blood, and shakes a chain
In a most hideous and dreadful manner:
You have heard of such a spirit; and well you know,
The superstitious idle-headed eld
Receiv'd and did deliver to our age,
This tale of Herne the hunter, for a truth.

Sample Program Theme: The Invention of Hugo Cabret by Brian Selznick

This and the following two programs provide fully fleshed-out outlines based on the program template. The first two focus on specific books, and the third on the work of a specific author.

PROGRAM TITLE
The Invention of Hugo Cabret Book Club

TOPIC
Read-aloud with focused activities based on ideas suggested by the book.

TARGET AUDIENCE
Ages eight–twelve

IDEAL AUDIENCE SIZE
Eight–twelve

LENGTH OF PROGRAM
Sixty–ninety minutes per week; nine sessions,
either twice per week or weekly

SETUP TIME
Varies by week, but typically fifteen minutes

PREPROGRAM TIME
Have supplemental materials in place twenty minutes prior to start time
for children who arrive early and need something to peruse.

GOALS AND OBJECTIVES FOR THIS SPECIFIC PROGRAM
- Develop literature appreciation
- Discover technologies
- Learn about the history of cinema

Description

Each session begins with reading out loud a portion of *The Invention of Hugo Cabret*. A suggested breakdown of the book over nine sessions is included below. The read-aloud is followed by a focused activity suggested by the book. At the end of each session, participants contribute to a blog about their experiences with the book and the program. Activities can include the following:

- Introduce the films of Georges Méliès.
- Watch films mentioned in the book.
- Invite a guest artist to teach the cross-hatching technique used by Brian Selznick in the illustrations.
- In groups, plan a story to tell in pictures. Use digital cameras to create the story in photos, which can then be posted on the blog.
- Invite a guest magician to teach basic magic tricks.
- Learn about automata, and create a paper automaton.
- As a final event, watch Martin Scorsese's movie *Hugo*, based on the book, and discuss how the book compares with the film.

Materials and Preparation

BOOKS READ OR PRESENTED
- *The Invention of Hugo Cabret*, by Brian Selznik, Scholastic, 2007

Supplemental Books: Drawing
- *Learn to Draw Now!* by D. C. DuBosque, Peel, 2000
- *You Can Draw Anything*, by Kim Gamble, Allen and Unwin, 2012
- *Drawing Made Easy: Realistic Textures*, by Diane Cardaci, Walter Foster, 2007
- *Lifelike Drawing with Lee Hammond*, by Lee Hammond, North Light, 2005

Supplemental Books: Magic
- *Big Book of Magic Fun*, by Ian Keable, Barron's, 2005
- *Magic Tricks*, by Cynthia Fitterer Klingel, Compass Point, 2002

Supplemental Book: Automata
- *Automata and Mechanical Toys*, by Rodney Peppe, Crowood, 2002

Supplemental Books: Digital Photography
- *Flotsam*, by David Wiesner, Clarion, 2006
- *Photography for Kids! A Fun Guide to Digital Photography*, by Michael Ebert and Sandra Abend, Rocky Nook, 2011
- *Digital Photo Magic*, by Alan Buckingham, Dorling Kindersley, 2005

- *The Kids' Guide to Digital Photography: How to Shoot, Save, Play with and Print Your Digital Photos,* by Jenni Bidner, Sterling, 2011
- *Digital Photography for Teens,* by Marc Campbell, Thompson Course Technology, 2007

ACTIVITIES, CRAFTS, GAMES, MEDIA, AND SOURCE FOR EACH

- Flying Pig paper animation: www.flying-pig.co.uk/content/shop-front
- DVD: *Hugo,* directed by Martin Scorsese, Paramount, 2011
- DVD: *Learn Magic with Lyn,* Lyn Dillies, 2005
- Website: Franklin Institute: www.fi.edu/pieces/knox/automaton/index.html
- Automata blog: http://dugnorth.com/blog/labels/Paper.html
- Paper model automata for purchase: www.c0014cats.biz/page2.htm

FILMS BY GEORGES MÉLIÈS ON DVD

- *Méliès the Magician,* Facets Multimedia, 2001
- *Georges Méliès: First Wizard of Cinema, 1896–1913,* Flicker Alley, 2008
- *A Trip to the Moon,* Flicker Alley, 2012

OTHER FILMS MENTIONED IN THE BOOK

- *Safety Last*—Harold Lloyd
- *Clock Store*—Disney Silly Symphony
- *Paris qui dort (Paris Asleep)*—Rene Clair
- *Le million (The Million)*—Rene Clair
- *The Kid*—Charlie Chaplin
- *Sherlock Jr.*—Buster Keaton
- *The Little Match Girl*—Jean Renoir
- *Zero de conduite (Zero for Conduct)*—Jean Vigo
- *Les quatre cents coups (The 400 Blows)*—Francois Truffaut
- *Sous les toits de Paris (Under the Roofs of Paris)*—Rene Clair

SUPPLIES NEEDED

Paper, pencils, scissors, glue

EXTRA STAFF NEEDED

Perhaps one other staff member during technical portions of program

EQUIPMENT NEEDED

Computers—every session; digital cameras last two sessions

ROOM SETUP

At one side or half of the story room, provide pillows and beanbags for children to sit on for the read-aloud and discussion portion of the program. For the activity portion, use a reserved bank of computers or use a special set of laptops in the story room. Tables may also need to be set up in the story room for some of the response activities.

CORRESPONDING EXHIBIT OR DISPLAY

Display books listed above. Only display those relevant to the session plus those from prior sessions.

CONTINGENCY PLANS

- Too few registrants (four or fewer): Contact those registered and encourage them to get a friend to register with them.
- Too many registrants (more than twelve): Take names, and if at least six are on the list, offer to split into two groups and run twice.
- Primary librarian unavailable to lead: Another librarian will be able to use these program plans as a substitute.
- Computers are down: Skip blog entry for the day. Share and discuss other print resources if planned online activities are not accessible.

PROGRAM PLANNING CALENDAR

Figure 3.4 (pp. 178-179) is a sample idea of how you might outline a nine-week after-school program for *The Invention of Hugo Cabret.* The discussion and blog-response sections have intentionally been left blank for the most part, as these will be driven by the dynamics of the children in the group. The activities are flexible and don't need to be done on the exact dates indicated. This is simply an idea of how you can spread the activities out over the length of the program. The format is adaptable for adding or subtracting days as well as changing which portions of the book to read in each session.

───────────────── *Poetry for* **The Invention of Hugo Cabret** ─────────────────

"The Clock of Life"
—Robert H. Smith

The clock of life is wound but once,
And no man has the power
To tell just when the hands will stop
At late or early hour.

To lose one's wealth is sad indeed,
To lose one's health is more,
To lose one's soul is such a loss
That no man can restore.

The present only is our own,
So Live, Love, toil with a will—
Place no faith in "Tomorrow"—
For the clock may then be still.

Figure 3.4 *The Invention of Hugo Cabret* **Planning Calendar**

Week	Read-Aloud Chapters	Story Events	Brief Discussion	Blog Response	Activity
1	Part I intro and 1–4	Toy vendor catches Hugo stealing and takes notebook from him. Hugo makes his clock rounds. Hugo follows toy vendor home, begging for notebook. He meets girl who says she will get notebook.	How do the pictures help the story? What questions do you have that you think will be answered later in the book?	What have these first few chapters made you curious about?	Introduce blog. Have children post an entry about themselves, plus the blog response.
2	5	Hugo takes out automaton. Background about Hugo's father and the fire at the museum. Hugo's life with his uncle. How Hugo retrieved automaton from ruins and decided to fix it.			Build a paper automaton using patterns from the Flying Pig website
3	6–7	Toy vendor shows Hugo a burned notebook. Girl says it isn't burned, and she will get it. Hugo starts working for toy vendor to try and get notebook back.			Guest artist teaches cross-hatching
4	8–9	Hugo fascinated by Papa Georges's card play. Meets Isabelle in bookstore, introduced to Etienne. Etienne buys Hugo the magic book he was about to steal. Hugo and Isabelle sneak into a movie. Hugo is fascinated by Isabelle's key necklace.			Guest magician

continued on page 179

Figure 3.4 **The Invention of Hugo Cabret Planning Calendar (continued)**

5	10–12	Papa Georges accuses Hugo of stealing, then he steals Isabelle's key as he leaves. Isabelle finds his secret apartment. They use the key to set the automaton in motion, and he draws a picture of the moon with a rocket in its eye.		Show the Méliès film *A Trip to the Moon* and possibly others as time allows
6	Part II 1–3	Automaton signs Georges Méliès name. Hugo's hand is crushed in the door when he tries to go home with Isabelle. They show the drawing to Mama Jeanne. Isabelle injures her leg pulling a box of Papa Georges's drawings from the armoire. Hugo starts investigating Papa Georges's secrets		Groups plan their picture stories and use digital cameras to create their stories
7	4–6	Hugo finds Etienne at the film academy, and they research the library for info on early movies. They find that George Méliès is assumed dead. Hugo arranges a surprise meeting. Hugo and Isabelle run the toy booth and discuss purpose.		Watch each group's picture story
8	7–9	Etienne and his teacher visit Papa Georges. They watch some of his old films; then Papa Georges comes in and takes the films and projector into the bedroom and locks the door. Hugo goes back to the station to get the automaton and hears a conversation about his uncle being found dead. Hugo is caught stealing and put in prison.		Watch other films mentioned in the book, or use time for picture-story digital-photo project
9	10–12	Hugo escapes and is recaptured. Papa Georges and Isabelle come to the train station to find him and take him home. Everyone attends an event in honor of George Méliès's life and work.	What does the title of the book mean? Does it have multiple meanings?	Watch *Hugo*, or do this as a separate tenth session

---

"Our New Robot" —*Anon.*

Last night Daddy bought us a robot
To help with the housework and whatnot.
It can cook fine cuisine
That is fit for a queen.
It can clean all the rooms
With its high tech brooms.
It can wash dirty clothes
Till they smell like a rose.
This robot is one of the latest inventions,
And I know Daddy had the best of intentions,
But it was so very expensive, you see,
The loan won't be paid till I'm thirty-three.
So Dad says we must take the greatest of care
Not to harm it or cause any wear and tear.
So Mom does the laundry and makes our lunch,
While Dad cleans the house and I serve the punch.
And what, you might ask, does the robot do?
He just sits by the window, enjoying the view.

This poem can be found in the following:
"Poems for Children," at www.poems4children.com/ournewrobot.html.

"My Robot" —*Shel Silverstein*

First line: "I told my robot to my biddin'"

This poem can be found in the following:
Silverstein, Shel, author and illus. *Falling Up: Poems and Drawings.* New
York: HarperCollins, 1996.

"From a Railway Carriage" —*Robert Louis Stevenson*

Faster than fairies, faster than witches,
Bridges and houses, hedges and ditches,
And charging along like troops in a battle,
All through the meadows the horses and cattle:
All of the sights of the hill and the plain
Fly as thick as driving rain;
And ever again in the wink of an eye,
Painted stations whistle by.
Here is a child who clambers and scrambles,
All by himself and gathering brambles;

Here is a tramp who stands and grazes;
And there is a green for stringing daisies!
Here is a cart run away in the road
Lumping along with man and load;
And here is a mill and there is a river:
Each a glimpse and gone for ever!

(See www.railwaybritain.co.uk/railway%20poems.html for more Stevenson poems.)

"In the Train"

—*V. De Sola Pinto*

I am in a long train gliding through England,
Gliding past green fields and gentle grey willows,
Past huge dark elms and meadows full of buttercups,
And old farms dreaming among mossy apple trees.

Now we are in a dingy town of small ugly houses
And tin advertisements of cocoa and Sunlight Soap,
Now we are in dreary station built of coffee-coloured wood,
Where barmaids in black stand in empty Refreshment Rooms,
And shabby old women sit on benches with suitcases.

Now we are by sidings where coaltrucks lurk disconsolate
Bright skies overarch us with shining cloud palaces,
Sunshine flashes on canals, and then the rain comes,
Silver rain from grey skies lashing our window panes;
Then it is bright again and white smoke is blowing
Gaily over a pale blue sky among the telegraph wires.

Northward we rush under bridges, up gradients,
Through black, smoky tunnels, over iron viaducts,
Past platelayers and signal boxes, factories and warehouses;
Afternoon is fading among the tall brick chimney-stacks
In the murky Midlands where meadows grow more colourless.
Northward, O train, you rush, resolute, invincible,
Northward to the night where your banner of flying smoke
Will glow in the darkness with burning spark and ruddy flame.

Be the train, my life, see the shining meadows,
Glance at the quiet farms, the gardens and shady lanes,
But do not linger by them, look at the dingy misery
Of all those silly towns, see it, hate it and remember it,
But never accept it. You must only accept you own road:
The strong unchanging steel rails of necessity,
The ardent power that drives you towards night and the unknown terminus.

"The Journey"   *—Harold Monro*

How many times I nearly miss the train
By running up the staircase once again
For some dear trifle almost left behind.
At that last moment the unwary mind
Forgets the solemn tick of station-time;
That muddy lane the feet must climb—
The bridge—the ticket—the signal down—
Train just emerging beyond the town:
The great blue engine panting as it takes
The final curve, and grinding on its brakes
Up to the platform-edge. . . . The little doors
Swing open, while the burly porter roars.
The tight compartment fills: our careful eyes
Go to explore each other's destinies.
A lull. The station-master waves. The train
Gathers, and grips, and takes the rails again,
Moves to the shining open land, and soon
Begins to tittle-tattle a tame tattoon.

They ramble through the country-side,
Dear gentle monsters, and we ride
Pleasantly seated—so we sink
Into a torpor on the brink
Of thought, or read our books, and understand
Half them and half the backward-gliding land:
(Trees in a dance all twirling round;
Large rivers flowing with no sound;
The scattered images of town and field,
Shining flowers half concealed.)
And, having settled to and equal rate,
They swing the curve and straighten to the straight,
Curtail their stride and gather up their joints,
Snort, dwindle their steam for the noisy points,
Leap them in safety, and, the other side,
Loop again to and even stride.
The long train moves: we move in it along.
Like an old ballad, or an endless song,
It drones and wimbles its unwearied croon—
Croons, drones, and mumbles all the afternoon.
Towns with their fifty chimneys close and high,

Wreathes in great smoke between the earth and sky,
It hurtles through them, and you think it must
Halt—but it shrieks and sputters them with dust,
Cracks like a bullet through their big affairs,
Rushes the station-bridge, and disappears
Out to the suburb, laying bare
Each garden trimmed with pitiful care;
Children are caught at idle play,
Held a moment, and thrown away.
Nearly everyone looks round.
Some dignified inhabitant is found
Right in the middle of the commonplace—
Buttoning his trousers, or washing his face.

Oh, the wild engine! Every time I sit
In any train I must remember it.
The way it smashes through the air; its great
Petulant majesty and terrible rate:
Driving the ground before it, with those round
Feet pounding, eating, covering the ground;
The piston using up the white steam so
The cutting, the embankment; how it takes
the tunnels, and the clatter that it makes;
So careful of the train and of the track,
Guiding us out, or helping us go back;
Breasting its destination: at the close
Yawning, and slowly dropping to a doze.

We who have looked each other in the eyes
This journey long, and trundled with the train,
Now to our separate purposes must rise,
Becoming decent strangers once again.
The little chamber we have made our home
In which we so conveniently abode,
The complicated journey we have come,
Must be an unremembered episode.
Our common purpose made us all like friends.
How suddenly it ends!
A nod, a murmur, or a little smile,
Or often nothing, and away we file.
I hate to leave you, comrades. I will stay
To watch you drift apart and pass away.

It seems impossible to go and meet
All those strange eyes of people in the street.
But, like some proud unconscious god, the train
Gathers us up and scatters us again.

Sample Program Theme: Chasing Vermeer *by Blue Balliet*

PROGRAM TITLE

Chasing Vermeer Book Club

TOPIC

Read-aloud with focused activities based on ideas suggested by the book.

TARGET AUDIENCE

Ages eight–eleven

IDEAL AUDIENCE SIZE

Fifteen–twenty

LENGTH OF PROGRAM

Sixty–ninety minutes per week; five sessions, either twice a week or weekly

SETUP TIME

Varies by week, but typically fifteen minutes

PREPROGRAM TIME

Have supplemental materials in place twenty minutes prior to start time for children who arrive early and need something to peruse.

GOALS AND OBJECTIVES FOR THIS SPECIFIC PROGRAM

- Develop art appreciation—the work of Vermeer
- Use pentominoes (a twelve-piece mathematical tool)
- Discover maps
- Learn about hidden messages and secret codes

Description

Each session begins with choral poetry reading followed by reading out loud a portion of *Chasing Vermeer*. A suggested breakdown of the book over the sessions is included below. The read-aloud is followed by a focused activity suggested by the book.

Materials and Preparation

BOOKS READ OR PRESENTED

Balliett, Blue. *Chasing Vermeer.* Illus. by Brett Helquist. New York: Scholastic, 2004.

SUPPLIES NEEDED

- Three of Vermeer's paintings as posters or large copies: *A Lady Writing, The Geographer,* and *The Artist in His Studio.*
- Oil pastels in bright and dark colors
- Watercolors in browns, blacks, and blues
- Drawing paper
- Black poster board on which to mount participants' finished "Vermeer" paintings
- Space to display their work at the library
- One lined poster board to display comments about Vermeer and the book to go with their artwork.

EXTRA STAFF NEEDED

Perhaps one other staff member during technical portions of program

EQUIPMENT NEEDED

Computers—every session

ROOM SETUP

At one side or half of the story room there will be pillows and beanbags for children to sit on for the read aloud and discussion portion of the program. For the activity portion we will go to a reserved bank of computers, or use a special set of laptops in the story room. Tables may also need to be set up in the story room for some of the response activities.

CORRESPONDING EXHIBIT OR DISPLAY

Display books and artworks listed above. Only display those relevant to the session plus those from prior sessions.

CONTINGENCY PLANS

- Too few registrants (four or fewer): Contact those registered and encourage them to get a friend to register with them.
- Too many registrants (more than twenty): Take names, and if at least six are on the list, offer to split into two groups and run twice.
- Primary librarian unavailable to lead: Another librarian will be able to use these program plans as a substitute.
- Computers are down: Skip blog entry for the day. Share and discuss other print resources if planned online activities are not accessible.

PROGRAM PLANNING CALENDAR

Figure 3.5 is a sample idea of how you might outline a five-week after-school program for *Chasing Vermeer*. The discussion, and blog-response sections have intentionally been left blank for the most part, as these will be driven by the dynamics of the children in the group. The activities are flexible and don't need to be done on the exact dates indicated. This is simply an idea of how you can spread the activities out over the length of the program. The format is adaptable for adding or subtracting days as well as changing which portions of the book to read in each session.

Poetry for Chasing Vermeer

"Vermeer" —*Howard Nemerov*

Taking what is, and seeing it as it is,
Pretending to no heroic stances or gestures,
Keeping it simple; being in love with light
And the marvelous things that light is able to do,
How beautiful a modesty which is
Seductive extremely, the care for daily things.

At one for once with sunlight falling through
A leaded window, the holy mathematic
Plays out the cat's cradle of relation
Endlessly; even the inexorable
Domesticates itself and becomes charm.

If I could say to you, and make it stick,
A girl in a red hat, a woman in blue
Reading a letter, a lady weighing gold . . .
If I could say this to you so you saw,
And knew, and agreed that this was how it was
In a lost city across the sea of years,
I think we should be for one moment happy
In the great reckoning of those little rooms
Where the weight of life has been lifted and made light,
Or standing invisible on the shore opposed,
Watching the water in the foreground dream
Reflectively, taking a view of Delft
As it was, under a wide and darkening sky.

This poem can be found in the following:
Inward Bound Poetry, at http://inwardboundpoetry.blogspot.com/
2008/12/751-vermeer-howard-nemerov.html.

Figure 3.5 **Chasing Vermeer Program Planning Calendar**

Week	Pages to Be Read Aloud	Story Events	Activity
1	86–88	Petra and Calder discuss facts on Vermeer that they find in books in the library.	Bring in a local art teacher to present information on Vermeer and his style. Have him lead the group through making their own art in the style of Vermeer. You can make simplified outlines of Vermeer paintings to give the kids a starting point. Kids can display their art at the library along with their opinions and facts about his artwork, or they can take them home.
2	74–75	Calder reads about secret codes in a book about Vermeer.	Hidden messages and secret codes, both online and on paper.
3	50–54, from chapter 6, "The Geographer's Box"	Calder uses his alphabet pentominoes to create anagrams and help him think while he contemplates a box that his grandmother has given him.	Anagrams and other word games. Write "Diamante" poems.
4	13, 84, discuss front cover art.	These pages explain Calder's fascination with pentominoes.	Pentominoes. Get plastic sets of pentominoes with puzzles to solve. Children can also color and take home their own paper set of pentominoes.
5	154–162, from chapter 16, "A Morning in the Dark"	Petra and Calder pretend to map the school as they search for the Vermeer painting.	Map making and geography games.

"Vermeer"
—*Stephen Mitchell*

First line: "She stands by the table, poised"

This poem can be found in the following:

Mitchell, Stephen. *Parables and Portraits.* New York: Harper and Row, 1990.

Parables and Portraits, at http://stephenmitchellbooks.com/poetry/parables-and-portraits.

"A Light Exists in Spring"
—*Emily Dickinson*

A Light exists in Spring
Not present on the Year
At any other period—
When March is scarcely here

A Color stands abroad
On Solitary Fields
That Science cannot overtake
But Human Nature feels.

It waits upon the Lawn,
It shows the furthest Tree
Upon the furthest Slope you know
It almost speaks to you.

Then as Horizons step
Or Noons report away
Without the Formula of sound
It passes and we stay—

A quality of loss
Affecting our Content
As Trade had suddenly encroached
Upon a Sacrament.

This poem can be found in the following:

Dickinson, Emily. *The Complete Poems of Emily Dickinson.* Boston: Little, Brown, 1960.

"Topsy-Turvy World" —*William Brighty Rands*

If the butterfly courted the bee,
And the owl the porcupine;
If churches were built in the sea,
And three times one was nine;
If the pony rode his master,
If the buttercups ate the cows,
If the cats had the dire disaster
To be worried, sir, by the mouse;
If mamma, sir, sold the baby
To a gypsy for half a crown;
If a gentleman, sir, was a lady,—
The world would be Upside-down!
If any or all of these wonders
Should ever come about,
I should not consider them blunders,
For I should be Inside-out!

Chorus
Ba-ba, black wool,
Have you any sheep?
Yes, sir, a packfull,
Creep, mouse, creep!
Four-and-twenty little maids
Hanging out the pie,
Out jump'd the honey-pot,
Guy Fawkes, Guy!
Cross latch, cross latch,
Sit and spin the fire;
When the pie was open'd,
The bird was on the brier!

This poem can be found in the following:
Poetry Foundation, at www.poetryfoundation.org/poem/239212.

"Friends" —*Abbie Farwell Brown*

How good to lie a little while
And look up through the tree!
The Sky is like a kind big smile
Bent sweetly over me.

The Sunshine flickers through the lace
Of leaves above my head,
And kisses me upon the face
Like Mother, before bed.

The Wind comes stealing o'er the grass
To whisper pretty things;
And though I cannot see him pass,
I feel his careful wings.

So many gentle Friends are near
Whom one can scarcely see,
A child should never feel a fear,
Wherever he may be.

"Puppy and I"

—A. A. Milne

First line: "I met a Man as I went walking"

This poem can be found in the following:
Milne, A. A. *When We Were Very Young.* Illus. by Ernest H. Shepard. New York: Dutton, 1961.

ADDITIONAL RESOURCES

Additional resources for a Chasing Vermeer program can be found at the following:

www.webenglishteacher.com/chasing-vermeer-lesson-plans.html
www.writingfix.com/Chapter_Book_Prompts/ChasingVermeer3.htm
http://adifferentplace.org/vermeer.htm

Sample Program Theme: Lois Lowry

There is no question that Lois Lowry is one of our finest contemporary writers. Her work, particularly the Anastasia books, is a terrific way to introduce realistic fiction. There is also a terrific connection to poetry, as Anastasia's father, Myron, is a published poet and a professor at Harvard. References to poetry can be found throughout the series. That will make it easy for you to find poetry to use in a series of sessions focusing on Lowry's books. The following list of read-aloud chapters could be used over a series of weeks. Note that page numbers refer to the original hardcover editions of the books.

TOPIC: **INTRODUCE ANASTASIA AND REALISTIC FICTION**
- *Anastasia Krupnik:* Description of Anastasia, p. 1
- Poetry is discussed in Anastasia's class, pp. 10–12

TOPIC: **NEW SIBLING**
- *Anastasia Krupnik:* Anastasia finds out there's going to be a new baby in her family, pp. 20–25
- Compare with Judy Blume's *Superfudge,* pp. 1–4
- Ask which book handles the topic more artfully.

TOPIC: **MOVING**
- *Anastasia Again:* Anastasia finds out that her family is going to be moving to a new house. The second section is very touching and bittersweet, as Anastasia looks for a way for her presence in her old house to be permanently recorded, pp. 1–6, 45–50
- Compare with the treatment of the same theme in *Superfudge,* pp. 26–29, 38

The following sections are simply "good parts" that are great fun to read aloud.
- *Anastasia Krupnik*: Washburn Cummings, pp. 44–47
- *Anastasia Again! Verdi's Requiem:* p. 64; Sam flashes his family: p. 141
- *Anastasia at Your Service*: Death scenes, pp. 1–3
- *Anastasia Ask Your Analyst*: Nicky Colleti, pp. 84–92; hamsters, chapter 6
- *Anastasia on Her Own:* Sam gets the chicken pox and uses a marker to try to connect the dots, pp. 47–49

In addition to her books about Anastasia, Lowry also wrote a series of books about her younger brother, Sam:
- *All About Sam:* Sam is born pp. 3–8; King of Worms, p. 74

Lowry has also written a series about the characters of J. P. and Caroline, children in a divorced family whose mother always threatens to send them to their father in Des Moines. The first book in the series has a couple of great read-aloud scenes.
- *The One-Hundredth Thing about Caroline:* Chapter 9: horrible, horrible, horrible, p 92. J. P. suggests hot-wiring a toilet seat: Hot-cross buns p. 96; (end of chapter 9).

Lowry has also written about a character named Gooney Bird Greene, a unique young lady with a teacher who knows just how to handle her uniqueness. The story of each book unfolds along with a project being undertaken by the class.

Lowry models a wonderful way of engaging children in learning. A couple of the books are about writing projects and would be perfect for a program where the entire book was read out loud with accompanying activities. Here is a list of the Gooney Bird Greene books in order of publication:

Gooney Bird Greene—Topic: Stories and Storytelling
Gooney Bird and the Room Mother—Topic: Theater and Putting on a Play
Gooney, the Fabulous—Topic: Fables
Gooney Bird Is So Absurd—Topic: Poetry
Gooney Bird on the Map—Topic: Geography and U.S. History
Gooney Bird and All Her Charms—Topic: Anatomy and Science

Lowry has an excellent website with lots of information at www.loislowry.com

Sample Program Theme: Suzanne Selfors

PROGRAM TITLE

Suzanne Selfors Book Club

TOPIC

Read-aloud with focused activities based on ideas suggested by Suzanne Selfors's books

TARGET AUDIENCE

Ages eight–twelve

IDEAL AUDIENCE SIZE

Eight–twelve

LENGTH OF PROGRAM

Sixty–ninety minutes per week; five sessions, either twice a week or weekly

SETUP TIME

Varies by week, but typically fifteen minutes

PREPROGRAM TIME

Have supplemental materials in place twenty minutes prior to start time for children who arrive early and need something to peruse.

GOALS AND OBJECTIVES FOR THIS SPECIFIC PROGRAM
- Develop literature appreciation
- Discover origami
- Learn about mythical creatures

Description

Each session begins with choral poetry reading followed by reading out loud a chapter from a book by Suzanne Selfors. A suggested list of books and chapters for a five-week session is included below. The read-aloud is followed by a focused activity suggested by the book.

Materials and Preparation

BOOKS READ OR PRESENTED

Selfors, Suzanne. *Fortune's Magic Farm.* Illus. by Catia Chien. New York: Little, Brown, 2009.

Selfors, Suzanne. *The Imaginary Veterinary: The Lonely Lake Monster.* Illus. by Dan Santat. New York: Little, Brown, 2013.

Selfors, Suzanne. *The Imaginary Veterinary: The Rain Dragon Rescue.* Illus. by Dan Santat. New York: Little Brown, 2014.

Selfors, Suzanne. *The Imaginary Veterinary: The Sasquatch Escape.* Illus. by Dan Santat. New York: Little, Brown, 2013.

Selfors, Suzanne. *Smells like Dog.* New York: Little, Brown, 2010.

FOR EACH PROGRAM

- Publicity needs to say that snacks are provided (e.g., "3:45–4:45, but come at 3:30 for snacks")
- Allergy warning sign on food table

SUPPLIES NEEDED

- For *The Lonely Lake Monster:* Paper, multiple copies of instructions, scissors
- For *The Rain Dragon Rescue:* Bowls, spoons (enough for one per participant), wax paper, chocolate, chow-mein noodles, dragon picture, hole punches, glue, crayons

EXTRA STAFF NEEDED

Perhaps one other staff member during technical portions of program

EQUIPMENT NEEDED

Computers—every session

ROOM SETUP

Classroom setup with tables and chairs sufficient for the number of participants

CORRESPONDING EXHIBIT OR DISPLAY

Display books listed above. Only display those relevant to the session plus those from prior sessions.

CONTINGENCY PLANS
- Too few registrants (four or fewer): Contact those registered and encourage them to get a friend to register with them.
- Too many registrants (more than twenty): Take names, and if at least six are on the waiting list, offer to split into two groups and run twice.
- Primary librarian unavailable to lead: Another librarian will be able to use these program plans as a substitute.
- Computers are down: Skip blog entry for the day. Share and discuss other print resources if planned online activities are not accessible.

PROGRAM PLANNING CALENDAR

Figure 3.6 offers sample ideas of how you might outline a five-week after-school program for five books by Suzanne Selfors. The suggested activities are flexible and don't need to be done on the exact dates indicated. This is simply an idea of how you can spread the activities out over the length of the program. The format is adaptable for adding or subtracting days as well as changing which portions of the book to read in each session.

Poems to Enjoy with *The Sasquatch Escape*

"I Think I'm Related to Bigfoot" —*Kenn Nesbitt*

First lines: "I think I'm related to Bigfoot, / though nothing has ever been proved"

This poem can be found in the following:
www.poetry4kids.com/poem-633.html#.U27–4y9LmZA.

"Bigfoot's Shoe Emporium" —*Kenn Nesbitt*

First lines: "At Bigfoot's Shoe Emporium / you'll find a dozen aisles"

This poem can be found in the following:
www.poetry4kids.com/poem-454.html#.U27_1i9LmZA.

"Bigfoot" —*David Ronald Bruce Pekrul*

He's ten feet tall with grizzled hair,
But he is very shy,
He roams the woods, the hills and vales,
His presence, they deny.

He walks at night among the hills,

Figure 3.6 **Suzanne Selfors Book Club Planning Calendar**

Week	Book	Pages to Be Read Aloud	Story Events	Snack	Activity
1	*The Imaginary Veterinary: The Sasquatch Escape*	1–12 (chapters 1 and 2 through page 12)	Ben sees the Wyvern flying through the sky and tries to figure out what he saw. Pearl sees it too and mouths the word *dragon*.	Pudding!!!! Chocolate, since Sasquatches like chocolate, and banana because Pearl likes banana.	Who made those tracks? Learn about the various footprints animals make. Compare various animal tracks.
2	*The Imaginary Veterinary: The Lonely Lake Monster*	76–83	Ben and Pearl leave the Imaginary Veterinary and find the Loch Ness Monster in the lake behind the building.	Jelly beans, especially kiwi and tropical flavors: coconut, pineapple, and mango. Sandwiches (perhaps sandwich cookies). Pearl likes sandwiches. Sunflower seeds (Pearl feeds her bird seeds).	Origami Nessie. Two versions: one simple and one harder.
3	*Smells like Dog*	56–67, excerpts	Homer sees a mysterious cloud and finds out that the dog he inherited from his uncle cannot smell.	Tomato soup	Treasure hunting with a compass. Have a staff member or volunteer lead an orienteering expedition both inside and outside the library in search of treasure. The group that finds the treasure gets a special surprise. Everyone gets candy.
4	*The Rain Dragon Rescue*	79–84 (chapter 9, "Dragon Food")	Ben and Pearl encounter the dragon. This is a great stand-alone chapter to read.	Sugary Fruity O's	Dragon droppings (no-bake cookies)
5	*Fortune's Magic Farm*	7–10	Isabell encounters the sea monster for the first time.	Apples	Magic potions

And sleeps throughout the day,
For that is how he can survive,
And keep them all at bay.

But that is not what he would choose,
If he could do it right,
But that is how they've treated him,
So now he roams at night.

He knows that if they captured him,
They'd tear him all apart,
To find out how he came to be,
And mark it on their chart.

A lonesome being, hard to spot,
But this is where he's put,
A creature sometimes called "Sasquatch,"
But most times called "Bigfoot."

Now, is this fantasy or real?
Well, only time will tell,
But until then he holds our gaze,
And keeps us in his spell.

Web Resources for *The Sasquatch Escape*

http://4h.uwex.edu/uphamwoods/programs/documents/AnimalSigns
LessonPlan.pdf

http://vailnaturenews.com/2011/06/lesson-plan-all-ages-how-to-identify
-animal-prints-and-track-patterns. Has a good PDF of different animal
track patterns.

www.dec.ny.gov/docs/administration_pdf/lpanimaltrack.pdf

www.dec.ny.gov/dectv/dectv116.html video

www.bear-tracker.com

http://nationalzoo.si.edu/Education/ClassroomScience/AnimalTracks/
v3%20Animal%20Track%20Student%20worksheets.pdf

http://media.animalnetwork.com/channelmedia/hobbyfarms/Animal
Trackfinal.pdf

http://filefolderfun.com/SecondGradeScience/AnimalTracks. Folder
games.

http://nwwoodsman.com/TrackingGame/TrackinGame.html.
Interactive games.

www.usborne.com/quicklinks/eng/catalogue/catalogue.aspx?cat = 1&

loc = uk&id = 3416.

http://library.thinkquest.org/J003192F/game.htm. Lost in the wetlands—identify tracks to follow them out to safety.

http://boyslife.org/hobbies-projects/funstuff/6662/animal-track-identification-quiz

http://raisingcreativeandcuriouskids.blogspot.com/2009/05/on-hunt-for-animal-tracks.html

http://evelyn_saenz.squidoo.com/animal_tracks. Identifying tracks in mud, snow, sand, etc.

Poems to Enjoy with *The Lonely Lake Monster*

"Too Messy for Nessie"   *—Donald Nelson*

First lines: "There's a terrible mess / On the shores of Loch Ness"

This poem can be found in the following:
   Johnstone, Julie. *The Thing That Mattered Most: Scottish Poems for Children.* Edinburgh: Scottish Poetry Library, 2006.
   Scottish Poetry Library, at www.scottishpoetrylibrary.org.uk/poetry/poems/too-messy-nessie.

"The Loch Ness Monster"   *—Fiona Lochhead*

Far from the dark and lonely shore
From the camera lights and the traffic roar
Nessie waits for a time to belong
The monster sings a lonesome song.

Dark ages have passed the frozen deep
And fish swim where the fossils sleep
But Nessie lives in a world that ends
To mourn the loss of time and friends.

She bides her time in the loch and still
Watching and waiting for hunters that kill
She casts sad eyes at the fisherman's net
The Loch Ness Monster extinct? Not yet.

She longs to see the lights of land
And feel the touch of beach and sand
But the world above is a dangerous place
Where she can never show her face.

And so she hides where they never know

And trawls the graveyard far below
Is there a place she can belong?
The monster sings her lonesome song.

"Nessie"   —*Elaine Magliaro*

First line: "What is living in Loch Ness"

This poem can be found in the following:
> http://wildrosereader.blogspot.com/2013/04/nessie-poem-about-loch
> -ness-monster.html

Web Resources for *The Lonely Lake Monster*
> www.activityvillage.co.uk/origami-loch-ness-monster
> www.activityvillage.co.uk/sites/default/files/pdf/origami_loch_ness
> _monster_instructions.pdf
> http://epicorigami.blogspot.com/2014/02/the-loch-ness-monster.html.
> Harder version!
> www.youtube.com/watch?v=j82nhICYUKQ

Poems to Enjoy with *Smells like Dog*

"Be Glad Your Nose Is on Your Face"   —*Jack Prelutsky*

First lines: "Be glad your nose is on your face, / not pasted on some other place"

This poem can be found in the following:
> Prelutsky, Jack. *Be Glad Your Nose Is on Your Face and Other Poems: Some of the Best of Jack Prelutsky.* Illus. by Brandon Dorman. New York: Greenwillow, 2008.

"Mother Doesn't Want a Dog"   —*Judith Viorst*

First lines: "Mother doesn't want a dog. / Mother says they smell"

This poem can be found in the following:
> Viorst, Judith. *If I Were in Charge of the World: And Other Worries.* New York: Aladdin, 1981.

"Digging for Diamonds" —*Kenn Nesbitt*

First lines: "I'm digging for diamonds. / I'm digging for gold"

This poem can be found in the following:
> Nesbitt, Kenn. *The Armpit of Doom: Funny Poems for Kids.* Illus. by Rafael Domingos. Spokane, WA: Purple Room, 2012.
> Kenn Nesbitt's Poetry4Kids.com, at http%3A%2F%2Fwww.poetry4kids.com% 2Fpoem-556.html%23.U2-U0S9LmZB

Poems to Enjoy with *The Rain Dragon Rescue*

"The Dragon on the Playground" —*Kenn Nesbitt*

First lines: "There's a dragon on the playground / who descended from the skies"

This poem can be found in the following:
> Kenn Nesbitt's Poetry4Kids.com, at http%3A%2F%2Fwww.poetry4kids.com% 2Fpoem-556.html%23.U2-U0S9LmZB
> Nesbitt, Kenn. *When the Teacher Isn't Looking: And Other Funny School Poems.* Illus. by Mike Gordon. Minnetonka, MN: Meadowbrook, 2005.

"Dragons" —*George W. Link*

> A Dragon is a special thing, unique to its creator,
> Some look like a serpent or a toothy alligator.
> Some have tails and wings and horns, while others have none at all,
> Some are absolutely huge, while others very small.
> I think that each displays a certain person's point of view,
> And what each means is something that's completely up to you.

This poem can be found in the following:
> Dragon Poetry at: www.tooter4kids.com/MedievalTimes/dragon_poetry .htm
> Teufelchen75cbeepworldde Blog at: http://teufelchen75c.beepworld.de/ dragonpoems2.htm

"My Invisible Dragon" —*Kenn Nesbitt*

First line: "I have an invisible dragon"

This poem can be found in the following:
> www.poetry4kids.com/poem-654.html#.VCIZ2OdaP-M

"I Wish I Had a Dragon" —*Shel Silverstein*

First lines: "I wish I had a dragon / With diamond-studded scales"

This poem can be found in the following:
Kenn Nesbitt's Poetry4Kids.com, at http%3A%2F%2Fwww.poetry4kids.com%
2Fpoem-654.html%23.U2-ZSi9LmZA

Web Resources for *The Rain Dragon Rescue*
www.freekidscrafts.com/wp-content/uploads/chinese-dragon-pattern.jpg
www.billybear4kids.com/holidays/ChineseNewYear/MakeADragon/
dragonHeads.shtml
www.pinterest.com/lakekowell/paper-dolls

Poems to Enjoy with *Fortune's Magic Farm*

"November" —*Alice Cary*

The leaves are fading and falling;
The winds are rough and wild;
The birds have ceased their calling—
But let me tell you, my child,

Though day by day, as it closes,
Doth darker and colder grow,
The roots of the bright red roses
Will keep alive in the snow.

And when the winter is over,
The boughs will get new leaves,
The quail come back to the clover,
And the swallow back to the eaves.

The robin will wear on his bosom
A vest that is bright and new,
And the loveliest wayside blossom
Will shine with the sun and dew.

The leaves today are whirling;
The brooks are all dry and dumb—
But let me tell you, my darling,
The spring will be sure to come.

There must be rough, cold weather,
And winds and rains so wild;

Not all good things together
Come to us here, my child.

So, when some dear joy loses
Its beauteous summer glow,
Think how the roots of the roses
Are kept alive in the snow.

"The Crossed Apple"   —*Louise Bogan*

I've come to give you fruit from out my orchard,
Of wide report.
I have trees there that bear me many apples.
Of every sort:

Clear, streaked; red and russet; green and golden;
Sour and sweet.
This apple's from a tree yet unbeholden,
Where two kinds meet,—

So that this side is red without a dapple,
And this side's hue
Is clear and snowy. It's a lovely apple.
It is for you.

Within are five black pips as big as peas,
As you will find,
Potent to breed you five great apple trees
Of varying kind:

To breed you wood for fire, leaves for shade,
Apples for sauce.
Oh, this is a good apple for a maid,
It is a cross,

Fine on the finer, so the flesh is tight,
And grained like silk.
Sweet Burning gave the red side, and the white
Is Meadow Milk.

Eat it, and you will taste more than the fruit:
The blossom, too,
The sun, the air, the darkness at the root,
The rain, the dew,

> The earth we came to, and the time we flee,
> The fire and the breast.
> I claim the white part, maiden, that's for me.
> You take the rest.

This poem can be found in the following:
Poemhunter.com, at www.poemhunter.com/poem/the-crossed-apple.

Sample Program Theme: Wendelin Van Draanen

PROGRAM TITLE
Wendelin Van Draanen Book Club

TOPIC
Read-aloud with focused activities based on ideas suggested by Wendelin Van Draanen's books

TARGET AUDIENCE
Ages eight–twelve

IDEAL AUDIENCE SIZE
Eight–twelve

LENGTH OF PROGRAM
Sixty–ninety minutes per week; four sessions, either twice a week or weekly

SETUP TIME
Varies by week, but typically fifteen minutes

PREPROGRAM TIME
Have supplemental materials in place twenty minutes prior to start time for children who arrive early and need something to peruse.

GOALS AND OBJECTIVES FOR THIS SPECIFIC PROGRAM

- Develop literature appreciation
- Discover computer animation
- Learn about the causes of bullying and how to prevent it

Description

Each session begins with choral poetry reading followed by reading out loud a chapter from a book by Wendelin Van Draanen. A suggested list of books and chapters for a four-week session is included below. The read-aloud is followed by a focused activity suggested by the book.

Materials and Preparation

BOOKS READ OR PRESENTED

> Van Draanen, Wendelin. *The Gecko and Sticky: Villain's Lair.* Illus. by Stephen Gilpin. New York: Knopf, 2009.
>
> Van Draanen, Wendelin. *Sammy Keyes and the Art of Deception.* New York: Knopf, 2003.
>
> Van Draanen, Wendelin. *Sammy Keyes and the Hotel Thief.* New York: Knopf, 1998.
>
> Van Draanen, Wendelin. *Shredderman: Secret Identity.* Illus. by Brian Biggs. New York: Knopf, 2004.

FOR EACH PROGRAM

- Publicity needs to say that snacks are provided (e.g., "3:45–4:45, but come at 3:30 for snacks")
- Allergy warning sign on food table

SUPPLIES NEEDED

- For *The Gecko and Sticky: Villain's Lair:* coloring sheet with fun facts about geckos, crayons
- For *Sammy Keyes and the Art of Deception:* drawing paper, pencils, colored pencils, white erasers
- For *Sammy Keyes and the Hotel Thief:* binoculars, yarn, and tape; scavenger-hunt lists; pencils; perhaps one other staff member during technical portions of program
- For *Shredderman: Secret Identity:* scratch lesson, pencils

EQUIPMENT NEEDED

Laptops—*Shredderman* session

ROOM SETUP

Classroom setup with tables and chairs sufficient for the number of participants

CORRESPONDING EXHIBIT OR DISPLAY

Display books listed above. Only display those relevant to the session plus those from prior sessions.

CONTINGENCY PLANS

- Too few registrants (four or fewer): Contact those registered and encourage them to get a friend to register with them.
- Too many registrants (more than twenty): Take names, and if at least six are on the waiting list, offer to split into two groups and run twice.
- Primary librarian unavailable to lead: Another librarian will be able to use these program plans as a substitute.

- Computers or software not available for *Shredderman*: Use small sticky notepads to make flip-book animation.

PROGRAM PLANNING CALENDAR

Figure 3.7 offers sample ideas of how you might outline a four-week after-school program for four books by Wendelin Van Draanen. The suggested activities are flexible and don't need to be done on the exact dates indicated. This is simply an idea of how you can spread the activities out over the length of the program. The format is adaptable for adding or subtracting days as well as changing which portions of the book to read in each session.

Figure 3.7 **Wendelin Van Draanen Book Club Planning Calendar**

Week	Book	Pages to Be Read Aloud	Story Events	Snack	Activity
1	*Sammy Keyes and the Hotel Thief*	Prologue and chapter 1 up to the point where Sammy Waves	Sammy sees a crime in progress through her binoculars.	Ice cream cones to go along with Double Dynamos.	Binocular relay and scavenger hunt.
2	*Sammy Keyes and the Art of Deception*	Excerpts from chapter 2. Chapter 12, pages 26–29 and 139–41	Sammy, Hudson, and Grams walk through the art gallery and discuss the paintings and are interrupted by a bandito with a gun. Later, Marissa and Sammy discuss the paintings and which ones they like.	God-like macaroni and cheese with salsa.	Explore abstract art and realism with a local art teacher. Learn to draw an eye.
3	*The Gecko and Sticky: Villain's Lair*	pages 1–5, and 53–54	Dave Sanchez discovers that his gecko, named Sticky, can talk.	Freaky frijoles dip.	Live gecko. Questions and answers with a gecko owner.
4	*Shredderman: Secret Identity*	Excerpts from pages 1–6	Nolan talks about his bully and nemesis, Bubba Bixby.	Jell-O cups, orange slices	Program your own simple animation using Scratch.

Web Resources for Wendelin Van Draanen programs

www.randomhousekids.com/brand/sammy-keyes/activities
www.teachingbooks.net/tb.cgi?aid=535

Activity guides are also available at the liveoakmedia.com site. Enter Wendelin Van Draanen in the search box, and the listings for the audiobooks include download links for PDF files.

Poems to Enjoy with *Sammy Keyes and the Hotel Thief*

"Raccoon Rex" —*Ruth Donnelly*

I walk by night, in darkness.
I sneak without a sound.
I overturn the garbage can.
Oh! What a treat I've found!

I grab the picnic sandwiches.
(I haven't yet been seen.)
I take my bounty to the brook,
And wash it squeaky clean.

I creep up to the campers' tent
And snatch a hot dog bun.
The campers yell. They scream and shout.
But I'm just having fun!

A mask of fur around my eyes,
A smile upon my face,
My paws can open garbage cans.
I move with stealth and grace.

I steal from people's garden plots,
From porches and from decks.
Yes, I'm a fearless bandit—
And my name is Raccoon Rex!

"Ice Cream" —*Steve Hanson*

First line: "I've replaced my bed with/an ice-cream machine"

This poem can be found in the following:
www.glowwordbooks.com/blog/2014/01/21/short-kids-poem-ice-cream

"Brand New Shoes" —*Kenn Nesbitt*

First line: "I bought a pair of brand new shoes"

This poem can be found in the following:
   www.poetry4kids.com/poem-602.html#.VEUxMRY010Y

"Bleezer's Ice Cream" —*Jack Prelutsky*

First line: "I am Ebenezer Bleezer"

This poem can be found in the following:
   www.poemhunter.com/poem/bleezer-s-ice-cream

"Spying on My Neighbor" —*Violet McDonald (age 11)*

   I've been spying on my neighbor for ages,
   If he drives in or out I see,
   It took me a year and a half to find out
   My neighbor was spying on me.

"Untitled" —*Gary Soto*

First line: "I once tried to steal from Charlie's Market"

This poem can be found in the following:
   http://poetryforchildren.blogspot.com/2007/04/happy-birthday-gary
      -soto.html
   Wilson Edward E., and Joyce A. Carroll, eds. *Poetry after Lunch: Poems to
      Read Aloud.* Spring, TX: Absey, 1997.

Poems to Enjoy with *Sammy Keyes and the Art of Deception*

"It's Abstract" —*Sean Kelly*

First line: "It seemed at first, a colour burst"

This poem can be found in the following:
   www.poetrysoup.com/poems_poets/poem_detail.aspx?ID=127684

"Art Is Hard" —*Gareth Lancaster*

First line: "Painting's really difficult"
This poem can be found in the following:
   www.fizzyfunnyfuzzy.com/poem/art_is_hard

"Painting Feelings" —C. J. Heck

First line: "How do I paint happy?"

This poem can be found in the following:
www.poemhunter.com/poem/painting-feelings-children
http://poemsabout.com/poet/c-j-heck

"I Went to the Farm Where Spaghetti Is Grown" —Greg Pincus

First lines: "I went to the farm where spaghetti is grown / In rows of long vines in a field of its own"

This poem can be found in the following:
http://gottabook.blogspot.com/2009/04/gregory-k-i-went-to-farm-where
.html and www.nowaterriver.com/poetry-month-2012-greg-pincus

"Arthur the Artist" —Kenn Nesbitt

First line: "I'm Arthur. I'm an artist, and I love to paint and draw"

This poem can be found in the following:
www.poetry4kids.com/poem-626.html#.VEU3zBY010Y

"Skateboarding" —Pene Burkey

First lines: "When I go rolling on my skateboard, / I feel the wind blow on my face"

This poem can be found in the following:
www.poemhunter.com/poem/skateboarding

Poems to Enjoy with *The Gecko and Sticky: Villain's Lair*

"The Gecko" —Alexander Nderitu

First line: "Poised halfway up the wall, the gecko watches me"

This poem can be found in the following:
http://alexandernderitu.blogspot.com/2011/04/gecko-poem.html

"Komodo Dragon" —Kris Wilson

First lines: "It sneaks and slithers, / It growls and hisses"

This poem can be found in the following:
www.poetry.com/poets/95261-Kris%20Wilson/205169-Komodo-Dragon

"Acrostic" —*Alice Morris*

> Great at walking on walls,
> Even upside down I never fall.
> Collecting the sun's heat
> Keeps me feeling sweet.
> Overall, I'm a little lizard trying to look cool.

"The World's Fastest Bicycle" —*Kenn Nesbitt*

First lines: "My bicycle's the fastest / that the world has ever seen"

This poem can be found in the following:
> www.poetry4kids.com/poem-381.html#.VEU4qhY010Y
> www.ridethenation.org/3800-mile-bicycle-blog/bicycling-is-poetry
> -in-motion

"My Foot Fell Asleep" —*Kenn Nesbitt*

First lines: "My foot fell asleep / right inside of my shoe"

This poem can be found in the following:
> www.poetry4kids.com/poem-379.html#.VEU5HhY010Y

"The Testimony of Sriwilai" —*Chang Liu*

First lines: "I, Sriwilai / gobbler of ants and fruit flies"

This poem can be found in the following:
> http://runpoemrun.wordpress.com/tag/testimony

Poems to Enjoy with Shredderman: Secret Identity

"I'm a Superhero!—A Silly Poem" —*C. M. Dixon*

First line: "I'm a superhero and I can prove it"

This poem can be found in the following:
> http://jakedogstories.blogspot.com/2013/08/im-superhero-silly-poem.html
> www.goodreads.com/author/show/5782819.C_M_Dixon/blog

"Bystander" —*Katie Niekirk*

I saw her in the morning
She threw her books in the dirt
But it's none of my business.

I saw her in the afternoon
Crying alone in the bathroom.
But it's none of my business

I saw her walking home
They followed her, throwing insults
But it's none of my business

I saw her every day
They did too, kept on and on and on
But it's none of my business.

I didn't see her today
She gave up, couldn't deal with it
She's gone

She's left school
She's happy now
It was my business.

This and other bullying poems can be found in the following:
www3.hants.gov.uk/childrens-services/childrenandyoungpeople/bullying/
bullying-professionals/ab-poems.htm

"I Am" —*Laura*

I am the person you bullied at school,
I am the person who didn't know how to be cool.
I'm the person that you alienated
I'm the person you ridiculed and hated.

I am the person who sat on her own,
I am the person who walked home alone
I am the person you scared every day,
I am the person who had nothing to say.

I am the person with hurt in his eyes,
I am the person you never saw cry.
I am the person living alone with his fears,
I am the person destroyed by his peers.

I am the person who drowned in your scorn.
I am the person who wished she hadn't been born.
I am the person you destroyed for fun.
I am the person, but not the only one.

I'm the person whose name you didn't know.
I am the person who just can't let go.
I'm the person who has feeling too.
I am the person just like you.

Make a stand. Wear a band.

This and other anti-bullying poems can be found in the following:
www.stclares.ie/anti_bullying_poems.html

"Shame: A Poem about Bullying"   *—Anon.*

There's a girl at school
We teased today.
Made jokes and called her names.
My friends all laughed,
Called it harmless fun,
Said it was just a game.

But now I'm home
Feeling terrible inside,
Long gone that thoughtless grin.
How will I face her
Tomorrow at school?
I wish I hadn't joined in.

"If I Could Be a Super Hero"   *—Steve Lazarowitz*

First line: "I don't think I could be Superman"

This poem can be found in the following:
www.authorsden.com/visit/viewpoetry.asp?id=106653
http://englishtime230.weebly.com/4/category/poetry/1.html

Chapter 4

Literature I Like to Share with Children

—•—————————•—

Baum, L. Frank. "The Magic Bonbons," "Project Gutenberg—Baum's American Fairy Tales," at http%3A%2F%2Fwww.gutenberg.org% 2Ffiles%2F4357%2F4357-h%2F4357-h.htm%23bonbons

This is a lesser-known story, unlike anything with which readers of Baum's Oz books may be familiar. Claribel gets a box of magic bonbons that she is told will give her the talents necessary to succeed onstage. High jinks ensue when the bonbons are mistakenly taken home by another little girl, named Bessie Bostwick. She and her parents eat them, and all of a sudden, they are performing piano sonatas like a concert pianist and singing like Metropolitan Opera stars.

Bridwell, Norman. *How to Care for Your Monster.* New York: Scholastic, 1970.

This book, by the author of the *Clifford the Big Red Dog* books, tells children how to keep and care for a large variety of monsters. Why have a pet when you can have a monster?

Clifford, W. K. "The New Mother," in *Anyhow Stories, Moral and Otherwise and Wooden Tony, and Anyhow Story: Reprinted from The Last Touches.* New York: Garland, 1977.

This is the scariest story I know. Written originally as a didactic morality tale to scare children into behaving, it has a raw power that transcends the didactic intent.

Copp, Jim. "Mrs. Goggins and the Gorilla," In *Jim Copp, Will You Tell Me a Story? Three Uncommonly Clever Tales.* Illus. by Lindsay Harper Dupont. Orlando: Harcourt, 2008.

Jim Copp's quirky stories first appeared on much-loved LPs between 1959 and 1971. This book collects three of his best-known stories, including "Mrs. Goggins and the Gorilla," about a school teacher and a man in a gorilla suit who interrupts her class. This is perfect for students to perform. Three other favorites can be found on Jim Copp and Ed Brown's recordings, which are now available on CD at playhouse records.com. Try "The Frogman," "The Dog Who Went to Yale," and "The Cow and the Kitty Cat." "The Dog Who Went to Yale" is a rhyming story about a dog that has the most remarkable longest name in the world. "The Frogman" is a story that will get younger children hopping like frogs. "The Cow and the Kitty Cat" is also great for younger readers. In the story, Cow and Kitty Cat move into a new house and try everything out. The doorbell rings, and a group of barnyard friends are there to celebrate with them.

Dahl, Roald. *The Gremlins: A Royal Air Force Story.* Milwaukie, OR: Dark Horse, 2006.

This obscure story by Roald Dahl was planned as an animated film by Walt Disney. A book was published with illustrations by Disney artists, but the film was never made. The basic preface is that the "gremlins" that get in the works of Royal Air Force planes are actually real. If you are doing any programming with any of Dahl's books, add this in the mix. It's short enough to read aloud.

Edmonds, I. G. *The Case of the Marble Monster and Other Stories.* New York: Scholastic, 1961.

Great stories to read aloud from the Japanese tradition. All of them are tales of Ooka, the wise judge of ancient Japan. My favorite is "Ooka and the Stolen Smell," which Tucson Puppet Works, in Arizona, turned into a lovely puppet show.

Feiffer, Jules. *A Barrel of Laughs, a Vale of Tears.* New York: HarperCollins, 1995.

This is a favorite read-aloud particularly because the author talks directly to the reader. Prince Roger has a gift for making people laugh, and as he embarks on his quest, he'll make your kids laugh as well.

Hitchcock, Alfred. "The Mystery of the Seven Wrong Clocks." In *Alfred Hitchcock's Solve-Them-Yourself Mysteries.* Illus. by Fred Banbery. New York: Random House, 1963.

This story lends itself well to reading aloud and then seeing if the children can solve the mystery. Kids may not know who Alfred Hitchcock was, but they will appreciate the challenge this mystery provides.

Nixon, Joan Lowery. *The House on Hackman's Hill.* New York: Scholastic, 1990.

Jeff and Debbie get trapped in the old house on Hackman's Hill when they go in search of a stolen mummy that may be alive.

Scieszka, Jon. "Each Sold Separately," In *Noisy Outlaws, Unfriendly Blobs, and Some Other Things That Aren't as Scary, Maybe, Depending on How You Feel about Lost Lands, Stray Cellphones, Creatures from the Sky, Parents Who Disappear in Peru, a Man Named Lars Farf, and One Other Story We Couldn't Quite Finish, so Maybe You Could Help Us Out,* by Ted Thompson and Eli Horowitz. Illus. by Lane Smith. San Francisco: McSweeney's, 2005.

This is a very short story in which two children communicate with each other using only advertising slogans and other memes. Have children identify each phrase and find the source.

Scoppettone, Sandra. *Suzuki Beane.* Illus. by Louise Fitzhugh. Garden City, NY: Doubleday, 1961.

Suzuki Beane is the child of a beat poet and sculptor living on Bleeker Street in New York City. Suzuki tells her story in first person in sixties vernacular and writes poetry, too. This is a short book that would be easy to read aloud. You can use it to encourage children to write their own poetry or even create their own art. They will love Louise Fitzhugh's (*Harriet the Spy*) illustrations.

Seeger, Pete, and Charles Seeger. *The Foolish Frog.* Illus. by Miloslav Jágr. New York: Macmillan, 1973.

If you want to incorporate music into your program, this story by the late, great Pete Seeger is the way to do it. It's a song, and it's a story. Kids will have fun learning the song and perhaps even acting like the foolish frog.

Zolotow, Charlotte. *The White Marble.* Illus. by Deborah Kogan Ray. New York: Crowell, 1982.

This is the beautiful, atmospheric story of two children, John Henry and Pamela, who share a brief magical moment in a park, highlighted by the discovery of a white marble. This would work well as a dramatization, perhaps in a real park. Or it could also be filmed.

INDEX

—•————————•—

Titles of poems and rhymes are shown in quotes.
Titles of books are shown in italic. *f* denotes figures.